Alan Lane is Artistic Director of Slu[...] company based in the oldest survi[...] Slung Low specialise in making large-scale productions in non-theatre spaces with community performers at their heart. During the Covid crisis, the company was the ward lead for social care referrals in Holbeck and Beeston, nearly 8000 homes in South Leeds. They ran a non-means tested self-referral food bank from March 2020 to June 2021. Lane was awarded a British Empire Medal for services to South Leeds during the crisis.

'This is an amazing story of remarkable people doing their very best in an unprecedented time for the world. This book demands that we revise our ideas about what theatre companies are for, what community art can be, and what people really need to live a full and productive life. Read this and be challenged and uplifted!' *Ian McMillan*

'I've never met Alan Lane, but I get the impression from his social media that he's not a man to flinch. So it wasn't a surprise that this memoir of a pandemic year, like his responses to the challenges it threw up, is both unflinching and uncompromising. He brings humour and humanity to the stories he tells and is simultaneously realistic about how things are and visionary about how they could be. The pandemic exposed the vast divides between those who have and those who don't, but Alan and Slung Low decided to tell a different story, and then to do whatever they could to make it true. At times challenging, yet always inspiring, *The Club on the Edge of Town* captures that story: the best of us, in the worst of times.' *Baroness Deborah Bull*

'Direct, honest and completely compelling; Alan's story is more than just a memoir of the pandemic, it's a manifesto on how to make the world a better place. It's the story of two worlds thrown together in the toughest of circumstances, trying to love, help and understand each other. What could be more relevant to our times!' *Sophie Willan*

Words on the book from a selection of members of The Holbeck.

'This is where we live, where we work and I finish the book, not despondent that the effects of the pandemic are far from over, but reminded Alan that there are, as you describe, "ordinaries, powerful enough and capable enough of making moments of profound change." And we will keep on, keeping on and yes, we will indeed go again tomorrow, hopefully still with soft hearts and definitely with slightly harder feet! *Laura Hodgkinson: Charity Leader, Kidz Klub.*

'The book is full of great stories. Of course it is – it's about Holbeck. Alan paints a picture of Holbeck and its residents that I recognise. Sometimes impoverished, battered by events, funny, resilient, diverse, often down, but never out.It's a terrific read, at turns a thriller, as Slung Low takes on local bureaucracy on one side and club members on the other. It's full of 'small p' philosophy, politics and most of all compassion. This isn't a book about individual heroes, although the feats achieved are heroic. It's a book about leadership and mobilising networks and partnerships and it points to how difficult that can often be.' *Jeremy Morton: Editor, South Leeds Life.*

'This book doesn't just tell the story of a food bank providing a vital service, or of a cruel benefits system created to keep people in poverty. It also serves as a manual for how to run a theatre company in a locality fraught with so many problems and barriers which can keep people from ever attending a live performance. It offers a glimpse of how, if we all work together and try our hardest to understand each other, then little by little we can change the world. It's about tons of white bread but it's about roses too.' *Claire Graham: Coach, Holbeck Moor FC*

'Often funny and often sad, but always brutally honest... This is the story of hard graft to build (often reluctant) trust with communities that feel unheard. But at heart it is a story of hope. That change can be made. That all of us are powerful. That we can all be storytellers, if we step up to the plate.'
Adam Ogilvie

'*The Club on the Edge of Town* is an extraordinary read. It's a celebration of a big, optimistic dream that if we could all just get along and help each other things would be better. However, it's also a frank account of why it's so very hard to make that work in the real world. It's a book that bolsters your hope for humanity whilst giving you a sharp reality check about just how selfish and self-destructive we humans can be. Not only that, this book is a provocation for those working in the arts. It challenges us to stop kidding ourselves about 'audience engagement' in big, expensive, unwelcoming buildings and to actually take the art to audience. And, most importantly, not to expect to be thanked and lauded for it.'
Lisa Holdsworth: Chair, Writers' Guild of Great Britain.

Alan Lane

THE CLUB ON THE EDGE OF TOWN

A Pandemic Memoir

Salamander Street

To Davidbaby,
For whom everything is done. Always.

'Now look, your grace,' said Sancho, 'what you see over there aren't giants, but windmills, and what seems to be arms are just their sails, that go around in the wind and turn the millstone.' 'Obviously,' replied Don Quixote, 'you don't know much about adventures.'

— Miguel de Cervantes, *Don Quixote*

FOREWORD

I read *The Club on the Edge of Town* in one sitting. I should have been doing something else, but I couldn't put it down. It made me want to head straight to Holbeck and work for Alan Lane. Everybody in the arts should read this book. So should everyone else. It's a page turner with all the heart of Alexander Zeldin, Ken Loach and Mike Leigh combined.

It is a book fuelled by love and delivered with an urgency deserving of that love. Love, in its most practical form, is the offer of food when you are hungry, not only 'food when you are hungry' but food which *nourishes*. There is no virtue signalling, no sanctimony. There is no time for that. This is what it means to be an artist, a citizen, a company. It's all in a list of three beliefs. To find out what they are, and how they work, enter *The Club on the Edge of Town*. The doors are open and the new neons are lighting up the night sky. There is a stone, there is always a stone flying through the air, hurtling towards the neon. Alan asks the question, 'what does the person who threw the stone need?'

But this is not a guide. This is the memoir of a place, of every town, village, or city we live in. I absolutely love this book and Slung Low and Alan Lane and the arts. There is hope! Thank you, Arts Council. Taxpayers' money well spent. Give him more.

Lemn Sissay, January 2022

INTRODUCTION

I urge you to read this book; you will not be disappointed. On the contrary, you will be uplifted, amused, frustrated, informed, perplexed and then uplifted again by Alan Lane's story of how a theatre company called Slung Low met the Holbeck working men's club.

I first met Alan several years ago when Slung Low was still based in five railway arches. Along with Judy and Olivia from my office, we went to visit, curious to find out what it was all about, and ended up having lunch in a beautiful Airstream caravan. I realised that day that I had met someone of remarkable energy and determination, and those same qualities exude from every single page of this memoir.

It's a most unusual love letter to the community of Holbeck and the people who live in it, and Alan tells it like it is. It is also a tale of relentless activity and practicality.

Holbeck working men's club almost closed and it was only because of the efforts of a group of dedicated local residents that The Holbeck – the oldest working men's club in the country – survives, nay thrives, to this day. This book is about the part that Slung Low played in making this happen.

As the tale unfolds, the theatre folk and the club committee began by circling each other rather warily. There were some differences of view over social distancing and the location of a rather unsightly bike shelter, but the partnership was well worth it. At the end of the book, a woman turns back to look at Alan one day as she is leaving the club and says 'we know that if Slung Low weren't here this place would definitely have closed by now.'

Alan has a wonderful gift of observation and his description of epic battles – notably a fight in the carpark after a child's first communion celebration party – will have you shaking your head in bewilderment.

We see the practicality when Covid and lockdown hit and Alan and his team turned their hands from putting on performances to running a food bank as if it was the most natural thing in the world (I now see how Alan's training as an army reservist helped to make lots of things happen).

With zeal, energy, cheerfulness and a wilful refusal to let bureaucracy and obstacles get in the way, the team helped to feed many people in Holbeck over the months. And all the while, they tried to live by their principles.

First, be useful. Second, be kind. And third, everyone gets what they want and no one gets to stop anyone else getting what they want.

The first two principles are very sound. The third proves to be a bit tricky, as we discover, not least because this is a book written against the backdrop of Brexit, which by definition was all about some people getting what they wanted and others not.

The characters are beautifully observed and there is a generosity to the portraits painted. There is also raw honesty about a community where poverty still stalks too many homes and families, and from time to time we are rightly invited to rage against the unfairness of it all and the cruelty of the benefits system.

To his great credit, Alan refuses to paint the one-dimensional picture of Holbeck that others sometimes do because they do not know it. Holbeck is full of people with talent, hopes, dreams, aspirations and stories to tell

– wonderful stories – and we learn that what motivates Slung Low is the desire to light the creative spark that is within each of us.

And where does that come from? There's a wonderful tale about Alan's childhood. He grew up on an RAF base in Germany and his mother knew he was both precocious and interested in music. She went to the office and asked if she could have a piano for her son. It turned out that pianos were available but only for the sons and daughters of officers rather than other ranks (Alan's dad was a corporal). Undaunted, his mother asked again and the man at the piano office said he would try although he added, 'look, there's no point in getting your son's hopes up. Don't be giving him ideas above his station. It's not like he will be able to make a living out of it.'

Oh, how wrong he was. Why? Because while bureaucracy and rules can on occasion crush aspiration, this story reminds us that hope and determination are, in the end, far stronger and will vanquish all. And while there are no perfect answers in an imperfect world, if you're looking for inspiration as how to navigate a way through life and its vicissitudes, then this is a very good place to start.

Hilary Benn
MP for Leeds Central

NO ONE GETS TO STOP OTHER FOLK GETTING WHAT THEY WANT

The referral phone rings. It's mid-September 2020 so we're delivering around 200 food parcels a week to families. In the last six months we've transformed ourselves from an outdoor theatre company into a foodbank working out of the oldest working men's club in Britain. Anyone who needs food in our South Leeds ward rings our number and we commit to getting food to them that day. And that phone is ringing. I answer.

'Is that the foodbank at the club?'

It's a woman ringing, furious that someone is trying to sell one of our food crates in a nearby pub.

'It's disgusting.'

'How much was he selling it for?'

'£20.'

'Don't buy it. You get one for free here.'

'Not the point.'

'What's the point?'

'He shouldn't sell it, he's taking from someone else.'

'He isn't. We're not going to run out of food.'

'But he shouldn't be selling it.'

'He isn't selling it. He's trying to sell it. No one round here is going to buy that for £20.'

'It isn't worth £20.'

'Exactly. And everyone knows they can get their own for free.'

'I've taken a picture of who it was.'

'I know who it was.' I didn't need a photo. It was one of our regulars, a dozen homeless (or nearly homeless) men who come every couple of days. Not for a full food parcel, but for the bits of it that they don't need an oven to eat. Because they don't have an oven. Or any electricity to power it even if they had one.

'Well, why did you give it to him then?'

'Because when he can't sell it, he'll probably eat some of it and that's my job.'

'It's madness.'

'Yes, but I didn't make this situation, I'm just trying my best.'

'I don't think it's right.'

'None of it is right.'

A pause. A hesitation and then...

'Will you be delivering my parcel as normal Alan?'

'Of course I will.'

'Can you put some salad in?'

'If I've got it.'

'Thank you.'

'Thank you for giving me a heads up about the selling.'

'It's just not right.'

'Folk are desperate.'

'Yes.'

And then she's gone. I make sure there's some salad in her box when it goes out later that day.

There are three clear values that Slung Low operates by.

Be useful.

Be kind.

Everyone gets what they want, but no one else gets to stop others getting what they want.

They're simple. My five-year-old son can understand them. But if they're committed to fully, especially when it's difficult, simple values like these can get you in to the sort of trouble that shift deep-seated assumptions and behaviours. They can lead to a theatre company becoming a foodbank in the middle of a global pandemic for example.

But to understand how all this happened, we have to start with the basics, an introduction.

TERMS OF REFERENCE: AN INTRODUCTION

Slung Low is a theatre company which specialises in making large-scale outdoor shows with casts of hundreds of people, normally in city centre locations in the north of England and with lots of fire and special effects.

We are part of the National Portfolio of Organisations that the Arts Council England manage. Which means Slung Low are given money every year to do their work from the public purse. In Slung Low's case that's £185,000. That sounds a lot, and it is a lot, but Slung Low is one of the smallest regularly funded theatre companies – but not the smallest.

We have worked out of Holbeck for ten years. Holbeck is a small inner-city ward of South Leeds. It has unusually high levels of deprivation. It is a mix of white, black and Asian working class who have lived in the area for a long time, and more recent communities who have come to the country in the last few years, often but not always from Syria, Afghanistan and Iraq.

That's probably all you need to know to get started.

THE CLUB ON THE EDGE OF TOWN

Slung Low had been based in railway arches in Holbeck since 2010. A little way from the houses in the area, we had taken over these five tatty arches and turned them into a rehearsal room and makeshift performance space, available to anyone who had need of it. It was called The Holbeck Underground Ballroom – the HUB.

And things had gone okay. We'd operated a Pay What You Decide policy on all shows and classes from the beginning: people pay what they decide after the event. At first people were unconvinced, some even mocking – 'naïve little fuckers' we were called by one visitor.

But after a few years the Pay What You Decide policy's impact on the types of people arriving at the HUB was obvious – people from communities and places that rarely, if ever, engaged with the arts were regularly turning up.

Now, nearly a decade on there's barely a cultural institution that isn't engaged in some similar, Pay What You Decide/Can/ Feel scheme. It has become mainstream. Being naïve is a useful thing sometimes.

Thanks to the quality of the visiting shows, selected for years by the brilliant programmer Porl Cooper, and the national press attention given to our schemes like Pay What You Decide, the HUB always punched above its weight. Which, given it was five railway arches in South Leeds without heating and several colonies of rats, is hardly difficult but it was the little venue that could and loved by many.

Despite this success, a constant failing was that we could never convince as many of the Holbeck residents to come to shows and classes as we wanted to. To get from where people lived to the HUB you had to walk through some horribly dark and dingy parts of town – and through the red-light district. But other than this, the HUB was a successful example of what a group of artists could do with a little money and a load of determination – a scrappy, interesting, engaging theatre studio so cold each audience member was handed their own hot water bottle on the way in.

In the middle of 2018 Network Rail had just sold its entire railway arches portfolio to a hedge fund, who had started removing businesses in London by putting their rents up 400%. At the HUB we'd had the annual fire inspection five times in six months and were starting to get the impression that our long-term future was not best served by trying to stay within the arches.

At the same time, I was rehearsing a kid's play – the stage version of *Tabby McTat* by Julia Donaldson – in the upstairs room of the nearby working men's club, The Holbeck.

The club was in financial difficulties. It owed a lot of money to the brewery Carlsberg Tetley and had been run for a number of years by a group of volunteers who cleaned, served behind the bar and did the books. They had managed to save the club from bankruptcy when many had gone to the wall through their commitment and hard work, but they were tired.

It's a lovely big room upstairs at the club, in need of some love at the time. That was true of most of the building outside of the main bar area. There was a two room flat with peeling wallpaper and no carpets, plenty of space and promise but the volunteers had concentrated on the two bar areas downstairs as they fought to turn the fortunes of the club around, leaving the rest of the building to fall into disrepair.

I really enjoyed rehearsing there. Big room, lots of windows, a decent kitchen downstairs.

Joanna, Slung Low's producer, saw the potential before the rest of us. She started talking to the club's committee about how much money they owed to the brewery.

Coincidentally in that same moment, we got our first Theatre Tax Relief payment. We'd made a big show with the BBC and the UK Capital of Culture Hull 2017 the year before and it had qualified us for a scheme the Government runs to encourage producers of theatre.

Theatre Tax Relief is the least progressive and democratic way of handing out public money to the arts – it rewards the already rich and commercial substantially more than anyone else. It's the naturally preferred way of supporting the arts if you are a small-state Tory: tax breaks and incentives for commercial ventures rather than the state subsidy of the Arts Council with its tendency to fund things that railed against conservative values.

More importantly in this instance, I had spent at least one year of arts conferences going around preaching the dangers of Theatre Tax Relief, reminding everyone, as Arts Council funding remained at a stand-still, that this was the least socially progressive way of supporting the arts. There was no way we could claim the money given everything that I had said about it. On this I was crystal clear. Unmovable. A man of determined principle.

'The Theatre Tax Relief payment is basically the same amount as the club owes,' Joanna informed me.

The theatre gods are not subtle beasts. I found a way to swallow my pride and we submitted our paperwork to the Government and awaited our payout.

We approached the club's committee with a proposal.

We would pay off the club's debts.

Return the deeds to the members.

Move in as managers of the bar.

Renovate the rest of the building and turn it over to cultural and community activity.

Guarantee the bar against loss (paying off any deficit at the beginning of each financial year to ensure it never falls again into debt).

And pay the Club's Managing Committee a £3k annual payment so they could continue with the community events that they regularly hosted.

But it had to be a unanimous members' vote in support. We wanted everyone's buy-in. There was to be a member's meeting one Sunday morning and a presentation followed by a vote.

Before the big vote, draft contracts would be negotiated between the two parties.

'Just write down whatever you want,' we told the committee, 'and we'll try to say yes to everything.'

In the end we did accept all the things they wanted to include in the contract. Except the committee's desire to be able to enter any room without notice: we had plans for workshops with young people and the vulnerable. We settled on forty-eight hours' notice.

And then the members voted. There were lots who had volunteered behind the bar who wanted to know if they could stay on. They could. From now on everyone working behind the bar would be paid the living wage. In actual fact, they didn't want the money. Some wanted to be able to contribute to this shared space they were a part of – and continuing to work behind the bar voluntarily was how they could do it. I was sympathetic to that. Locking in everyone's emotional investment was going to be the key to the whole thing working.

But there were some who wanted to retain the authority to go behind the bar whenever they wanted. We couldn't say yes to that. This was going to have to be a professional operation – owned by the members, managed by us – we couldn't have members just bimbling behind the bar after a few pints. I explained this to the room, heads started to shake, a rumbling in the ranks. It was the first sign that not everything was going to go the members' way.

But despite this speed bump the vote was unanimous.

We would take over on 7th January 2019. We now managed the oldest working men's club in Britain.

Our first act as managers would be to shut the place for three weeks, in order to have asbestos removed from the cellar.

THE CURSE OF RICHARD CURTIS

Many years ago, we had a project called The Knowledge Emporium. A beautiful, silver 1956 airstream caravan: like the ones Hollywood stars of yesteryear got changed in.

Inside the caravan was an old-fashioned sweet shop: jars full of sherbets and jellies and lollipops and striped paper bags. Outside the sweet shop caravan stood men and women in striped waistcoats, billowing dresses, bowties and bowling shoes. If you approached, they would explain that this was a sweet shop with a difference: it accepted only knowledge and not money. If you wrote a piece of knowledge – a fact, a story, a recipe, whatever you decided – in *The Big Book of Everything that We Know,* which was stored in the caravan – then you could help yourself to as many sweets as you wanted. After a week of collecting, all that knowledge would be read out to an audience gathered outside the caravan before The Knowledge Emporium set off to another town.

It toured all over the country for years and proved to be wildly popular, in large part because people really like sweets, but also because they like being told they have something worth recording and saying out loud.

The first time we ever did it was with a little theatre in Notting Hill called The Gate. The caravan was parked on the bottom of Portobello Market. They hated us there from the very first moment.

The caravan arrived and I set up. The surrounding shopkeepers and residents were mostly a study of disinterest, if not occasionally open disdain. I couldn't understand it. What had we done? That first morning no one approached: a silver caravan, a man in a bowtie and bowling shoes and not one person was interested in what it was all about.

There was a launderette opposite the caravan and a woman who looked like she was in charge. I approached.

'Hello!'

She ignored me.

'Hello! I'm from the caravan across the way.' I explain about the sweets and the knowledge book and the reading at the end of a fortnight.

'I'm going to stand outside that caravan all day every day collecting people's knowledge in return for sweets.'

'Yeah, we're not interested in that sort of thing.'

'Not interested in sweets?'

'You've just come here to steal our stories.'

'What?'

'You'll just steal what we tell you and make it into a movie or something.'

'I bet I won't.'

But there was no telling her. I have never in my life met someone who so viscerally hated Richard Curtis. The reality of Notting Hill – at least this bit we were in down the bottom of the market – was a world away from the not-that-old-at-this-point film *Notting Hill*. And the fact that her reality had been eradicated by that piece of fiction genuinely upset her. I talked to a few other people that morning – heading into their shops or catching them unawares – and they all said the same thing. Not necessarily with the same venom against Mr Curtis but the idea of outsiders – 'people like you' – coming in and taking something of the area and then leaving to tell the world a different story was genuine, firmly felt and the reason why no one would go within five metres of The Knowledge Emporium.

At first, I found the whole thing a bit silly. We'd spent weeks making this beautiful thing, the most non-aggressive, generous thing we could think of, and it was going to fail because of a Hugh Grant movie. Yet here it was. All that first day no one was coming near the place apart from a handful of tourists. But with time on my hands, I came to understand that it wasn't really to do with Hugh Grant – it was being written out of your own story, being unheard. For many good reasons, over many incidents, for many decades the people of this place had been promised much by folk who looked and sounded a lot like me, and none of them had really delivered. And as a result, they didn't trust me or what we were doing.

The next morning started the same way. A few withering glances as they opened up their cafes and shops. I settled in for another long day standing in front of a caravan being ignored.

Then it started to rain. Rain like the sky was angry. Absolutely huge drops smashing down and bouncing back off the ground again. I didn't move. I had promised to stand outside this caravan all day every day for two weeks. I hadn't said I'd only do it if it was nice weather.

The first hour passed. The rain beat down. I was wet. A large man in a waistcoat, bow tie and bowling shoes looks silly – but when he's drenched through, he is ridiculous.

Still I stood. Not out of any great moral certainty but because we said we would, and I couldn't think of a reason to break that promise. It kept raining.

After about ninety minutes the woman from the launderette came out with an umbrella.

'What are you doing?'

'Standing outside the caravan all day every day for two weeks.'

'This is so stupid.'

'Okay.'

I cannot express to you how wet I was. Like I'd been submerged in a bath.

'You're stupid.'

'Okay.'

She turned to go, walked a few steps, had a different thought, turned around and handed her umbrella to me and then ran back to her shop.

I took it. I hadn't promised not to use an umbrella.

It rained for another hour or so. I stood under my borrowed umbrella looking like a drowned candy-striped yeti. When it stopped there was some mocking cheers from the sandwich shop across the way. No Richard Curtis style moment of resolution for my wet self.

But that afternoon she came across from the launderette and into the caravan. 'I'm only doing this for the free sweets because I like sweets.' The rest of them followed over the next few days.

By the time the reading happened two weeks later all the local shop keepers were there, along with a healthy splattering of residents. It felt like we'd been there forever and only just arrived all at once. Which is always what it feels like when you stand in a place all day every day for a week or more.

The shorthand in Slung Low for keeping your promise no matter what it takes is Standing in the Rain. Communities like that one on Portobello Market, and in Holbeck, have been promised the earth many times and have got used to the perfectly reasonable excuses they're told as to why those promises can't be kept. The distrust that generates is destructive.

The only way to break the cycle is to keep your promise. No matter the cost. No matter how daft it makes you feel, no matter how inconvenient: you keep your promise, no matter what. Even if it means standing in the rain.

We had some way to go before they trusted us in The Holbeck. Thankfully there was plenty of rain coming.

BIG NIGHT IN

Closing for a few weeks immediately after taking over as managers was far from ideal, but there's no negotiating with asbestos. And we had asbestos in the cellar that had to come out so we could put a better cooling system in. The old system, a huge unit that rattled and sputtered, was a 1970s disaster movie waiting to happen. In the top floor flat, up two flights of narrow stairs, the windows were unopenable and double glazed. In the event of a fire you were meant to kick the window in and make a jump for it from the third floor. I put a 10lb sledgehammer and rope ladder next to the window. It was the best that could be done, and it wasn't much of a solution. All this being understood, reducing the likelihood of a fire seemed like the only sensible way forward. The old cooling unit was going to have to go.

We used the closure to get the rest of the building in shape. We used to have barn days at the HUB when repairs were regularly needed, and the level of finish was industrial enough to let everyone join in: with a bit of supervision the same idea could work here at the club.

So, for two weekends, artists we'd worked with and our audience members stripped wallpaper, painted walls and revarnished the bar. The gang quickly got the abandoned rooms back into shape. The flat would become dormitory accommodation for artists working in the region, an old office turned into a room for the children who came with their parents on a Sunday to play. It was great to see so many different types of people pitching in. Except the members. I couldn't help noticing that none of the established members were there. It should perhaps have been a warning of a disconnect but at the time I thought it a good sign that they trusted us to get on with the work in hand. After all, a small number of them had been doing this on their own for a long time; time for someone else to take on the graft.

Once all the asbestos was cleared out, all the mould treated upstairs and the place given a big spruce and clean we reopened with a mighty cabaret; Divina De Campo leading a seven-piece band in an evening of magicians, poets, improvisors and fire eaters. The place was heaving. 280 crammed into the big performance space with its new cabaret stage. The Chief Executive of the Arts Council England sat alongside the club's committee and local residents who had never set foot in the place before but who we'd managed to convince in.

It was a rare thing, a hit with all the different communities that had a stake in the club. Women, now in their seventies, who had come to events in their childhood spoke with tears in their eyes about how overjoyed they were that new life was being breathed into the place. If we could keep this up, then the whole thing might work.

DRAMATIS PERSONAE

S lung Low was founded in 2000 by Matthew David Scott and Alan Lane (that's me) as they were leaving the University of Sheffield. Nowadays it can take a long time to get a theatre company to the point where it can actually pay people a wage you can live on. And so it was with Slung Low, twelve years to be precise. But when that day arrived everyone was to be paid the same – no matter what their job. If the promise of making theatre being a team effort is real than the spoils must be equal. Now every member of the company is paid the average wage of the nation (£28,600) or £110 a day.

On the one hand, this amount of money for members leading a company with the national impact of Slung Low's is very low, if not an outlier alone.

On the other hand, when the members of the club found out this was how much each of us was paid, they could not believe it. Genuine disbelief that running a theatre company could be financially rewarded so well.

The gap between these two world views, both held in good-ish faith, is the gap between those who are looking to make marginal gains in the improvement of society and those who feel a disconnection from so much of the nation as to be in a constant state of disbelief or outrage. This gap, in one way or another, is where Slung Low has spent the last twenty years.

And over those years there have been many people who have joined and pushed the company on – brilliant people who came together principally to enjoy the shared endeavour of making theatre that rips disbelief from audiences in places you were never expecting. The producer Laura Clark who would put the company on some sort of competent professional footing, then go on to work for Jude Kelly and the National Theatre of Scotland, is one of a number of brilliant people who put their shoulder to the wheel for a few years before moving on to different challenges in other parts of the sector.

There are easier companies to be in than Slung Low. Outdoor theatre in the north of England requires the hardiness of a fell sheep. Working in Holbeck requires a social robustness not found in all theatre folk. And the company wage and the endless reinvention, changing of output, learning of new skills is thrilling and galvanising and exhausting. There are easier ways of earning money than this. And earning £28,600 is riches beyond compare for anyone who has spent their career working as a freelance artist in the north of England but substantially less than they might be used to if they've come from other sectors – and that starts to grind on folk too.

But whilst the pros remain more vivid in your mind than the cons, there are few alternatives as exciting. The roll call of brilliant Slung Low members over the years is impressive and so it was with the team that moved into the club.

At the heart of the company now sits, and has for seven years, the producer Joanna Resnick – daughter of an American teacher on the nearby United States Air Force base – she started life with Slung Low ten years before the move to the Holbeck as a week-long work placement. And then moved through every single development stage the company had. When Laura was ready to move on, the only possible sensible replacement to run the company was Joanna. It's rare this happens nowadays, almost an old-fashioned apprenticeship progression, but it means that at the beating heart of a company sits a financial and logistical mind steeped in the lessons learnt from the last decade.

Matt Angove – once a sound designer for the dance legend Matthew Bourne – has been with the company for as long as anyone can remember. Bringing his technical skills and patience to everything, he's the reason why the oldest working men's club in Britain has a much better sound and lighting system than anyone should ever be able to expect.

Two of the current team were with us fifteen years ago as actors before (as is so often the way in theatre) finding other careers; Ruth Middleton an accountant, and Sally Proctor a teacher. Both returned, bringing a set of skills from other professions to the team.

And the final member during the Covid year was Holbeck resident Ruth Saxton. Formerly a curator at the national children's museum Eureka, her arrival at the team was the first time that a Leeds United fan had ever been a part of the company. You wouldn't necessarily think that would make a difference.

But as I write this, I look out the window to see a large refrigerated food container in the car park, provided by Leeds United (and their sponsor Clipper). I also think of the large number of upcoming initiatives that we have with our noisy premier league neighbours. And we'd never had anything to do with them in the twenty years before.

Each of us have a profound effect on the whole – that's one of the best things about Slung Low.

For my part you only need to understand that I am the punk front man to their group of classically trained musicians. It's my job to put the collective effort and endeavour into a missile shaped statement. And when we find a roadblock that can't be worked around it's my job to put on the Hulk suit and disrupt the obstacles before us so that the problem is at least reconfigured into one that can be resolved. It's a hell of a job.

NEW PARTNERS

Every working men's club has a committee, voted in by the members, which supervises the managers of the club. Traditionally these committees are full of byelaws and benefits, life members and perks in return for their voluntary work as legal guardians and trustees. Think of it like the board of a charity that get paid in twenty-five pints a week. So, like being in the House of Lords then.

That's not how it works at The Holbeck. Long before we arrived, the committee had arranged themselves into a leaner, more practical group of people. Gone were the privileges hidden in labyrinthine standing orders; and in were a determined group of people who took on the responsibility of cleaning toilets, pulling pints and hoovering up after events.

The story goes that Ian Pickup – now the club's Vice President – was campaigning with Labour Councillor Angela Gabriel. That's right, Holbeck's ward councillor is called the Angel Gabriel: a terrifying and exceptional public servant. Holbeck, the place of magic and story.

Ian was campaigning with Councillor Gabriel when they knocked on the door of Club President Terry Nichols. In what we have since explained is an act of election fraud, Terry promised to vote for the Councillor if they helped him with the club.

The club – like almost all similar ventures in the wake of the economic downturn, and a general decline in drinking trends – was in financial difficulties. Ian, along with his husband Dennis Kitchen, promised to help the committee work their way out of trouble and attract new members to the club. In return the perks of being on the committee and stranglehold grip of archaic regulations would have to cease. No more free beer for starters.

Both Dennis and Ian were part of a Christian Fellowship and they – led by the three musketeers of Bill, John and Pete – collectively moved into the club and onto the committee and became vital parts of the operation.

So, the committee we inherited is a large group drawn from both communities; established club members and the Holbeck Christian Fellowship. Two dozen individuals all under the leadership of President Terry and Vice-President Ian. There was clearly tension between these two groups of people. In spite of that, they'd been running the club for years, undertaking all the menial tasks, and had managed to get it back to breaking even. There was even one year (as long as you didn't want to pay anyone) in which they made a profit which, if you took a look at the books, you would understand was no mean feat. It was, for all its schisms, a brilliant collaboration of at least two parts of the community with the crystal-clear mission to save the club from going under.

And it's with that committee that we had a first meeting as managers. The end of the second week of January 2019. We had been in just one week.

We'd just about managed to get our desks up and get the stocktaker in. And it was the stocktaker who had brought us some far-from-welcome news. So, we'd called an emergency meeting.

In the last week of December – the week before we took over – several hundreds of pounds had gone missing. Indeed, in the final quarter hundreds more was missing – both cash and stock.

The stocktaker was one the club trusted and had used for a long time. In the past couple of years, the regular stock take had shown the usual returns for a club our size: some wastage, the occasional cash discrepancy but all within the margin of error. And then, in the final weeks before the committee handed over responsibility for the club to us, someone had had away with stock and cash.

We asked the stocktaker to double check. He did. The same result.

And so, the first meeting of the committee, when all of us at Slung Low were still working out how to pour a pint without a seven-inch foam head, was going to involve me explaining to the only people with access to the money that lots of it had gone missing.

There was nothing for it but to tackle it head on.

I suspected that someone, or a group of people, saw new outsiders arriving splashing the cash around paying off debts and making improvements and thought that they were owed some of these fruits from the money tree for all their volunteer hours over the years. Which was annoying, and also understandable.

It was simultaneously true that we couldn't spare the time for an investigation to find out who exactly had done it – indeed it was likely to be impossible to ever be certain – and this absolutely couldn't be allowed to happen again. The money that had been stolen wasn't ours but the club's. And therefore, the members' money.

And we had recently stood up in front of many of them and promised to do our best to look after this shared thing.

So, things had to change. I explained to the committee that a large amount of money had gone missing and gone missing on their watch. That as their managers we were bringing this to their attention and committing to ensure it would not happen under our new management. I had ordered new safes, new locks on the doors and from now on only trained members of staff could go behind the bar. Everyone on the committee was very welcome to attend the training so they could go behind the bar, sign out a set of keys and so on. But not until they had attended the training.

I was pretty sure I had game-theoried the whole thing out: I anticipated some shouting and then agreement with my response to the challenge. I was, not for the first time with this group of people, entirely wrong.

The committee rejected the stocktaker's report. Therefore, there was no trouble, no need for these security measures. I couldn't understand it. It was their stocktaker. He'd been doing the job for years. I had been expecting some sort of breakdown in trust between them as it dawned on some of the committee that one of them had helped themselves to the fruits of their hard work. But they stood as one. There was a mistake in the stocktaker's report. Both of the reports.

In the end they relented about the security measures, allowing it as a surfeit of enthusiasm in a new manager. To this day they still reject the idea that money had gone missing. Even though it demonstrably had. It is literally not in the bank account.

We would still be chasing committee members out from behind the bar for months to come but our resolve was firm and in the end the changes stuck. Someone had stolen from the members of the club and that person had to be in that meeting. Some of those present would become our friends as the years went by, others would grow tired of our management and drift away but that first meeting of committee and management has always stuck with me. In a moment when the acceptance of the facts presented would have led to them scrutinising those they had been working with so hard for so long they simply chose not to accept the truth. It was a moment of collective denial in keeping with the times. It was brilliant practice for Brexit and Covid – both of which were on their way.

A BLUE PLAQUE

Hard on the heels of our big night in together, the cabaret so warmly received, we were told the great news that the club was to get its very own blue plaque.

The text on the club's blue plaque reads **Holbeck Working Men's Club. Originally established in 1871, these purpose-built premises officially opened on Easter Monday 1878. Built at a cost of £1,172 the club included rooms for refreshment, billiards and bagatelle and a lecture hall for 300 people. No other working men's club has been in continuous operation for so long.**

It was a moment of real achievement, particularly for Dennis and Ian who had campaigned hard for the club to play a bigger part in the community. They had had a vision for the club to become an arts centre and they had seen it happen and secured the club's financial future for as long as anyone could reasonably ask for. Now there was to be a blue plaque to commemorate the place.

There's something reassuring about a blue plaque: it makes things feel more certain and grounded somehow. To have been entered into the public record. A tiny part of your reality will live on, no matter what.

We were aware that there are few blue plaques to working-class culture, and we shouldn't let the moment pass without due celebration. It was agreed that we would organise an event to mark the unveiling. It was also agreed that Slung Low would pay for it because the club didn't have any money.

We set about rounding up friends and favours. We had a little makeshift stage we could put up out front and a sound system.

Hilary Benn is our MP and a reliable and enthusiastic supporter. He'd give a speech if the vote in Parliament on the Brexit deal went ahead in time, or was cancelled, either of which felt reasonably likely – so there was that.

Ian McMillan is one of the finest poets alive in Britain. And he was a friend of ours, and a fan of our Cultural Community College that he had come to teach at a few months before. Could he be persuaded to write a poem to mark the occasion? He enthusiastically agreed to help.

We wanted him to talk to some of the members about the history of the club and could think of no one better than Margaret Nutter. Margaret, along with her retired firefighter husband John, was a vocal member of the Committee. Her opinion of any new proposal was always the best sense of how the members generally would feel. She was fierce in her criticism when she felt something had been half-arsed, but her love of the club was real, her understanding of the good it did to people, and the support it provided, lived and authentic.

In those first weeks in charge of the club when we were removing the asbestos, I had given a focus to hand sanding the bar. Night after night I'd stay late and set about the bar top to get it gleaming. When we re-opened, I stood proudly in front of it knowing Margaret would be first in and waiting to see what she thought. She walked in, took one look around, pointed at me and said, 'these chairs are in the wrong order.' I learnt in that moment that it would take a lot to impress Margaret and that the chairs in the downstairs bar went red, blue, red, blue and not any other pattern.

I knew no better guardian of the club's soul and excitingly she really fancied the idea of talking to the Bard of Barnsley.

The poem Ian wrote is a beautiful piece of art. A triumphant example of the thing we aspire to at Slung Low: the moment when an exceptional artist meets the participation of community members and something amazing happens.

Holbeck's Never Ending Story by Ian McMillan

We all need a palace when we come in from a shift
We all need a big room that can give our hearts a lift
We all need a spot to meet our mates and have a laugh
And talk about the old times and say 'Here's a photograph
Of the club in 1946 and there's your mam and dad
Sitting in the same seats that the buggers always had;
Their parents came in here and their mams and dads and all
You can see the smoky shape of grandad's Brylcreme on the wall.

We can all remember how they queued on New Year's Eve
For hours in the freezing cold and folks might not believe
That we had waiters serving drinks; the concert room was full
Of people laughing, dancing, life was never ever dull
And workers wiped the dirt off, put on their frocks and ties
And laughed away the weekend with ale and tunes and pies
And the idea of a club is that people get together
Help each other through the sunshine and the heavy weather

We all need a palace but this palace almost fell
This building and its history could have been an empty shell
But six people rolled their sleeves up to save the Holbeck club
And it was hard and it was mucky it was lift and clean and scrub
It was order beer and pay for beer and make the windows gleam
And all these different people made themselves into a team
Now glory days are glory days but the past has been and gone
And the waiters fade, the big turns end, but Holbeck carries on

The oldest club in England, the doors still open wide
A matter of survival? Yes, but here's the thing: it's pride
Makes Holbeck what it is and a willingness to say
The future's where we're aiming from the springboard of today
We'll see you in a hundred years when we'll all still be here
The future's dancefloor shining and the future's glass so clear.
And let's march on together: we are Holbeck, we are strong
I'll tell you what: If we could sing we'd make this poem a song!

WHAT WE BELIEVE

We spend £500 million of public money in this country on the arts in England. Arts Council England give the Royal Shakespeare Company £14.98 million of all our money every year. Arts Council England give the National Theatre £16.7 million of our money. And there's £10.3 million to Opera North and so on until £500 million is spent.

They spend £185k of your money on Slung Low. We can talk about whether that specifically is good value another time.

Slung Low believe that given we spend £500 million of our money everyone in the UK should have access to the best possible cultural life. But we don't. We know that. There are so many places – many like Holbeck – that don't have access to any of the culture that money pays for. And certainly not to the best and most exciting parts of how it's spent. Priced out of mainstage theatre shows, made ignorant by marketing campaigns that fail to touch large swathes of the city, or excluded by public transport systems that find it improbable that anyone in a major northern city might want to catch the bus home after a performance of an evening.

This is true.

And it is intolerable. And it is cruel. To have a system which has built into it the idea that a child in Holbeck is not worthy of the joy that watching truly great art can bring, is not capable of meeting the quality of that and therefore is not worthy of it. It is cruel.

And so Slung Low are committed to doing what we can to correct that cruelty, and to dismantling that system whenever we get the chance – bit by bit.

What in reality this means is our commitment to being Holbeck's theatre, bringing as much resource to the cultural offer to the people of Holbeck and leveraging whatever cultural capital our reputation can to the area: practically we paid off the debts of the local working men's club so it didn't close and run everything we do at the club on a Pay What You Decide.

These are the things we believe. Because we believe them, we have done the things we have done.

BLUE ON BLUE PLAQUE

The blue plaque unveiling event was fast approaching. We were still working out how best to pull it all together. We'd made shows all over the world, in palaces and on national television but this one had more pressure on it than any that had come before. We were six months into managing the space and the honeymoon was over. The Committee, although happy not to be undertaking the physical labour of it all, were missing control over the daily decisions. Some members would stalk around the club trying to find where the cleaners (now paid) had missed, or order the bar staff to go and change this barrel or that. Things were bubbling to a head.

There had been an almighty argument over a bike shed of all things. As is so often the way, it's the small things upon which big rows often turn. The Committee had approved a bike shed outside the club which we'd found funding for so we could encourage people to bike here. But we hadn't discussed exactly where it was going. Without giving it too much thought I'd put it under the CCTV at the front of the building to improve the security. But that meant it stood out and proud in front of the building.

'It looks horrible!'

'We'd agreed we were going to get a bike shed.'

'It makes the place look like a community centre. It isn't a community centre, it's a bar!'

'Only for the last fifty years. It was a community centre long before it was a bar.'

Which of course only made matters worse. Our honouring of the club's history reflected the 150 years it had sat in the middle of Holbeck. The committee was honouring the club of their childhood, the club of their parents: Sunday drinking and bingo. Only a fool messes with that.

And, if truth be told, the bike shed was in the wrong place. A stupid decision for a theatre director. It was in the right place logistically, but the visual metaphor was all wrong. The powder coated round metal was all youth club and medical centre: not working men's club. We manage the most iconic building in the area, and I'd dumped a blue bike shed in front of it. That the Committee had agreed to it was neither here nor there, of anyone I should know better – I make pictures full of meaning for a living, right? And more importantly it looked like we were trying to stamp our mark on the place when really it had just been a decision made quickly and without enough thought.

It would be two more years before I found the money and excuse to move that bike shed somewhere else and for all that time the resentment bubbled.

But in the meantime, the unveiling of the blue plaque event was fast approaching.

'It's been written to be spoken out loud and even better if it can be sung,' said Ian McMillan of the poem.

Sally would be reading it at the event, but Ian McMillan had got us thinking.

Boff Whalley is a friend of the company, a brilliant writer, an extraordinary songwriter, he used to be in the band Chumbawumba and now leads Commoners Choir. Commoners Choir is a wonderful mass choir who sing their own songs about inequality and hope. They'd recently done a concert to celebrate the Kinder Scout mass trespass – an act of civil disobedience that would lead the country to the creation of national parks and the Pennine Way. If there was to be any group of people who would understand the importance of a working men's club blue plaque surely it would be them? Could they turn the poem into a song?

They could and they would, and also sing a bunch of songs of their own at the unveiling event.

Perfect. We arranged caterers and bought as much fizz as we could afford and started inviting people. Official invites went out to the city council and dignitaries on behalf of the club Committee.

On the day everyone came. It was a lovely day, sun high in the sky. The vote on the Brexit deal was delayed so Mr Benn could be there.

'I might boo him,' one of the very Brexity members said.

'Not if you want any more free drinks,' I said as I handed over a glass of champagne. I would keep the peace today if it killed me. Or someone else.

Sally read the poem beautifully and the crowd cheered and then Commoners Choir took to the stage and, there being very many of them, all around the stage. They sang songs raging against inequality, songs of hope, songs taking the mickey out of Boris Johnson. I looked up to see if I could see Mr Benn's face during that last one but he's a consummate professional and looked on with a neutral look of generic contentment.

Then everyone was in for a buffet and more free fizz.

By dint of one of those annoying theatre diary clashes that never lets us enjoy anything for too long we had to quickly strike the stage and leave everyone partying as we drove vans full of equipment down to London. The next night we were staging an outdoor cabaret in the middle of a South London high-rise estate. I had a 4am call in Covent Garden veg and fruit market to buy ingredients for the audience's dinner so was keen to get on our way so I could get my head down for a few hours.

We left everyone at the club tucking into cake, waved goodbye and hit the M1.

The next morning, as we cooked a three-course meal for one hundred people in a kitchen we'd built in the middle of a basketball court, I got an email from a Ward Councillor.

They'd received a complaint about the event the night before. An event they'd been invited to by the Committee of the club. The complaint came from the Committee of the club.

I tried to get to the bottom of it. Members of the Committee had written about how offended they had been at the political content of Commoners Choir's set. Particularly the bit when it was suggested that Boris Johnson's hair was so chaotic that you could behead him and stick his head on a stick and use it as a mop to clean up the mess he'd made of the country.

'I honestly had no idea that any of them were Tories,' I said to Matt as we frantically chopped carrots for one hundred portions of soup.

'It's not that. It's Brexit.' he replied. Ah of course, yes. Boris's Brexit.

I spoke to the discontented.

'I'm sorry that you weren't happy. I think Commoners Choir did a great job. They did it as a favour to us and because they believed in the thing being commemorated, the club.'

'There's no place at that event for politics. You ruined it with politics.'

'It was the unveiling of a blue plaque for a working men's club, it's all politics.'

'You know what I mean.'

'No I don't. Everything we do is politics. Paying off the debt of the club is politics. It's all politics.'

'We should have booed them when they started singing.'

'Yes! If there's ever anything on stage here that you find so offensive that you feel compelled to boo, then definitely boo. But beware, Boff Whalley is likely to boo you back.'

'How would you like it if me and my friends started a choir and sang songs about things that upset you!'

'Hand to god, you do that, and I will book you. Get rehearsing and I will put your first gig on here.'

That's not a principle ever likely to be tested. I know these men would never in a million years form a choir and sing any songs, let alone ones that upset me, but it would be good to have the commitment to programme them tested one day.

Somehow, we had gone from a bright sunny day of celebration to the Committee complaining to the authorities about an event. An event they not only hosted, but to which they had invited those same authorities. I could never have imagined it would be about this, but I knew that something was coming.

Aside from daft mistakes with bike sheds we had set everything the traditional members cared about in aspic. The bar and lounge were exactly as they had been, the beer prices frozen for a year, bingo still happened in hushed silence on a Sunday. But on the things that the traditional members didn't care about there had been a series of revolutions. The pub filled during the weekdays with classes and community groups, upstairs with rehearsing artists.

Before our arrival Saturdays took less than £100 across the bar. Ghost town. So now on a Saturday we filled the concert room with queer cabarets, Ghanaian weddings and a whole host of events by and for other communities in Holbeck who hadn't previously felt like they could come to the club.

One hundred new members had joined since we arrived: supporters happily paying membership dues to see the whole project succeed.

Those that had been here before were always going to feel some whiplash.

The established members and the Committee had got everything they asked for from our arrival. But they had grown increasingly unhappy (and vocal about it) that other groups also seemed to be feeling more and more at home at the club. The Boris Johnson song, and the cheer that it got from a large crowd that evening, had been the last straw.

Who would have thought it. In one of the safest Labour seats in the country that a music hall style gag song about using the mop-like hairdo of the Tory Prime Minister as an actual mop could cause so much trouble. But it did.

In the age of Brexit, no joke was deemed too silly to be ignored.

WHAT ARE YOU GOING TO DO
ABOUT IT?

The phone rings one morning and the woman on the end explains that she is a club member, and she needs to come down and see me – can she come down this morning? At this point, I'm so used to people just arriving in the office and shouting at me that I find the idea that someone has asked for an appointment to be delightful. Of course she can.

She arrives shortly after, a lovely woman called Mandy with her husband, Paul, in tow.

'Paul worked at Patisserie Valerie...'

Now I heard something about that on the radio this morning, what was it?

'...and they all got laid off this morning because it's gone belly up.'

That was it, Patisserie Valerie had laid off all their staff.

'I am so sorry to hear that. Terrible news.'

'What are you going to do about it?'

'What am I what?'

'Well, you've moved in here, we saw you on the telly the other day, and the paper. You're always talking about what you're up to. What have you got on?'

We weren't the only thing going on in Holbeck at that moment. But we were the noisiest. We are a theatre company – we can't even reopen a pub without press releases and documentary crews and fireworks. It was good that it was being noticed. But it had never occurred to me that someone would just walk in like this. But why shouldn't they? It struck me in that moment that this was a perfectly reasonable response. And it required something more useful than my open-mouthed dopeyness.

'What do you do Paul?'

'He's a chef.'

'Are you a good one?'

'He is.'

'I've got an important cabaret coming up. 200 people. Could you cook for all of them?'

'I'll do a tester for you.'

'Okay. We'll pay for both. Our rate is £110 a day will that work?'

It would.

The couple would do a brilliant job of the cabaret. And go on to use the kitchen for a business idea they had for afternoon teas and catering for wakes. They are some of my favourite people I met that first year. Fair, determined, hard-working: how Slung Low aspire to be.

We had never been based anywhere before where that would have happened. We ran a place people turned to for help when news headlines became part of their everyday lives. Even in the worst days to come, when some of the members became unhappy and the reality of running a useful space felt overwhelming, we held on to that knowledge. Where we were based now mattered to people. It was important. And in a moment of crisis, it was where people turned.

FINGERNAILS IN THE CAR PARK

The phrase 'Cultural Democracy' is currently in vogue. And with good reason, even though like all capitalised phrases it is used as a fig leaf for an awful lot of what we already know doesn't work, dressed up in new clothes. But at its heart it's about getting more people to feel ownership and power over their cultural life: let people decide what they want to do and help them do it, rather than the top-down organisation of culture we might be used to.

As we look out across the nation, and further afield, there is an undeniable discontentment. Whether it be the rise of populist gobshites to the highest office of America and the United Kingdom; or the current argument about flags and whether to shag or burn them, there is a sense of bubbling anger about many things. Smarter people than I have argued, and they are right, that this comes from a disconnect, a sense that the system we all live in does not care for them, does not consider them.

What is extraordinary is that all the different sides of this argument can feel like they are the hardest done by. Whether it be the conflicts around trans people and single sex spaces, the white working class and people of colour, Schrodinger's asylum seekers who come to steal our jobs and our benefits, or any of the other false dichotomies that have sprung up in the last twenty years, we are faced with narratives of how one group is being persecuted by another group – and it's usually the case that neither group has any real power.

As the old gag goes, the man with ten biscuits turns to the man with one biscuit and says, 'Watch out, I think there's a refugee arriving to steal your biscuit.'

The traditional rump of the club members – white men in their seventies, retired on pensions that allow them to drink in clubs and go on foreign holidays – believe themselves to be the most put upon parts of society. Even in this ward with visible, immediate, Victorian levels of poverty, this is their narrative. 'They want their country back', from whom is never really stated. 'They can't say anything nowadays', although exactly what it is they want to say is never actually said. We should have the freedom of speech to offend, unless it's to take the piss out of the Union Jack then you should be fired from whatever your job might be.

Standing before them and telling them to 'check their privilege' is not only tactically stupid, but also tone deaf to a community that, whilst far from being at the bottom of the pile, have been badly led, lied to, abused and overworked for generations.

Intellectually we might understand that there is privilege here to be checked, that – whatever their individual struggles and inequalities – there is systemic racism and sexism that they have benefitted from and their fellow citizens have suffered from. Yes, this is surely all true.

But the good faith required to have that conversation is long since dead in Holbeck and those that would wish to keep our discourse on other baser, less nuanced subjects have loud, confident voices.

The immediate flash to bang of tabloid emotion – I say this, you feel this – cannot be countered with delicate, patient conversation about giving up a little status and comfort to create a fairer society for all with people who feel as though (not unreasonably) that they have substantially less comfort than they were promised.

And in response to this situation, you need a strategy that shifts the ground on which these dichotomies are based. At Slung Low that is Cultural Democracy or, in something that feels less like it was named by cultural academics – 'Everyone gets what they want (and no one gets to stop anyone else getting what they want)'.

Or tactically – everyone can have the big room whenever they want.

In the past there was an hourly charge for the event room if you wanted to hire it for a private event. It didn't bring very much in annually and being a Pay What You Decide organisation, we got rid of that. Now you could pay what you decided, and therefore could afford (which might be nothing).

In the past, there was a cleaning deposit. A not insubstantial amount of money agreed previously and held in cash. As your event ended – 2am in some cases – the supervising member of the Committee would inspect the place, and if the standard had been met, you would be given the deposit back. The deposit amount could change according to the perceived risk of whether you would clean the place up.

If you were looking to create a subjective system designed to generate resentment and accusations of unfair treatment, you'd do well to find one better than this 2am tired and worse for wear one.

So, we got rid of that as well. After a lengthy and expensive trial of many hoovers, we found ones that were powerful enough to deal with the ancient carpet upstairs (do not bother with any fancy brand, the answer to your question is Henry Hoover – trust us). 'How bad could the mess get?' we thought, like the naïve fools we are.

Then we spread the word that anyone who wanted to use the Event Room would be welcome. A simple booking form (four questions) was all people needed to fill in to book the space.

The main public space in the area would be available to anyone. Yes, we would programme it with shows and events, but the majority of events upstairs would be members of the community doing what they wanted. Battle of the band events, political party fundraisers, award ceremonies, weddings of all sorts, first holy communions, men's support groups, parenting get-togethers: whatever people wanted. We would help with technical support, sound equipment, bar staff and whatever else was needed from us.

So, we hosted everything and anything. Plenty of things that we would not have chosen if we had the choice. But because of our principles we didn't, so we got on with it. Cultural Democracy. It's the people's palace, not ours. We said yes to everything and with very few exceptions (political party fundraisers mostly) the events were successful in their own terms.

'When people ask if you think arts funding in the UK is a good idea you remember that it was because of arts funding that your nan's eightieth birthday party could happen here, okay?'

Well, hopefully they remember. But more importantly we were connecting the dots. Our arrival at the Holbeck wasn't something happening TO them but rather one of the benefits of living in the UK, a country that believes in progressive and positive things like arts funding. Everyone getting what they wanted didn't harm anyone – the Ghanaian funeral had no negative impact on any other group, the care-leavers' dinner every Thursday took nothing away from anyone else.

All that had to happen for this to be true was that someone, us, had to make sure that the place was lovely for each and every group that used it. And this meant hoovering.

What we discovered was that every single group, every different race and every political persuasion that used the event room was incapable of taking food from a paper plate and getting it into their mouths without dropping much of it on the floor.

Every single one.

In fact, after months of hoovering, it occurred to me as the nation got more and more fractured around the oncoming Brexit that this might be the one issue we might all rally around. Sausage rolls, Bombay mix, cheese on sticks, chicken wings, peanuts... I have hoovered pounds and pounds of food from the floor of the concert room.

It's almost galvanising that in a community so often described in terms of its fractures, we had found the one thing that connected all the different parts of our community. They were all scruffy buggers.

To use the big room upstairs there were as few rules as possible. You didn't have to have the bar open, but you couldn't bring your own drinks, no exceptions. And we were drug free, no messing about with this. The whole Slung Low project, funding and artistic ambition, was reliant on this bar remaining open and I wasn't going to have it closed because some drongo at a wedding started doing sniff in the bogs.

A few months in we were asked if we would host a first holy communion celebration. Of course we would. I was secretly a tiny bit pleased. It was true that everyone was welcome, but this was my tribe at last, getting involved.

On the day the family put out the classic buffet of various beige carbohydrates and then went off to church and whilst we got the bar ready.

The family arrived back two hours later with a few guests in tow. Fewer than might be expected.

'There was a fight at the church, so a lot of the family aren't coming.' I was told by the mum. I've been there, I thought.

There was only one child in the room and she was wearing the white dress of someone who has just joined the Roman Catholic church. She was all on her tod. Poor kid.

Then the DJ begins. Techno music, a bold choice, starts up and the little girl starts dancing enthusiastically. There are less than two dozen people in the room, so I leave it with the bar staff and head to the office.

Two hours later and I'm called up by the bar. Brother of the father of the communicant is refusing to pay for his drinks unless the bar staff have a shot. Not unreasonably, our bar staff who like most of our staff were actors and directors and producers from the city's theatre scene between performance jobs, weren't having any of this nonsense.

'What's the problem?'

'I'm not going to pay for my round unless she has a shot.'

'She's at work, she doesn't have to have a drink.'

'You have it then.'

'Pal, I've not had a drink in over a decade, I have one now we have bigger problems than your unpaid bar bill.'

'SOMEONE HAS TO HAVE A SHOT!'

'Okay Scarface chill your beans. How much is his round?'

Twelve pound something the bar staff tell me.

'Okay pal, no one is going to do a shot for you.'

'You going to call the police? You going to make me pay?' I'm struggling not to laugh here. 'It's a first holy communion party, I'm not calling the police. I'm not fighting you. We're just not going serve you anymore. I think I'll manage to find the twelve quid.'

He looks confused.

'You're no fun!'

'I get that a lot.'

He throws a note and some coins on the bar and stomps off.

'What on earth is going on with this lot?' I ask the bar staff, who point to the dance floor.

I look up and realise exactly what is going on.

I find the mother and father of the little girl in the white dress who is still on the dance floor.

'Sorry to disturb. I'm going to ask you to tell all your guests who have taken drugs to leave immediately or I'm turfing you all out. Do you understand me?'

The father explodes. 'How dare you? I've never been so insulted. I should knock you out, how dare you?! What makes you think that anyone we know would take drugs!'

'Turn around and take a look.'

And behind him on the dance floor is his daughter – still in her white communion dress – dancing to the techno music. And next to her is a man in his late thirties, with his top off, also dancing to techno music and gurning like a marketing executive at the company Christmas do.

The father turns back to me. He makes his choice and the tension releases from his body.

'Okay fair enough, give me five minutes.'

'You've two. And I want them all gone,' I say pointing to two more idiots in the corner thinking they're in *Goodfellas* and not at a little girl's party on a Sunday afternoon. Nearly every man at the party walks out two minutes later, taking the opportunity to express themselves fully to me through my office window.

About three hours later I'm sat working in the office and there is an almighty crash bang and our Terence, one of the excellent actors who work behind the bar, comes running in. 'You better come outside and deal with this.'

The women from the party upstairs are now in the car park and fighting each other. The father is sat on the step of the club, barely able to keep his head up, shouting about how he doesn't want the party to end. The girl, who a few hours ago was being blessed by a priest, is stood watching on like something from a scene in a Ken Loach film. And the women are tied up in each other's hair and punching each other.

I'm weighing up the options of foam extinguisher or calling the police – both of which will extend my working day in ways I want to avoid – when the gentlemen thrown out earlier arrive on the scene. At least they've their tops on now.

They've come to fetch their partners. I ask if they can stop them fighting in the car park.

'It's easier to let them blow themselves out mate, I'm not getting involved in that,' one of them replies.

They're right. The fight ends a few minutes later. Some bits of hair, some nails on the car park but nothing more serious than a black eye. And then they start to make their way into town, made up or still sulking. They stagger away. The little girl following. The event is over. Time for the hoover.

'You okay boss?' asks Terence.

'Yeah. Just my tribe showing us all up eh.'

Cultural Democracy. The only way as a nation we're getting out of the binary mess we're in, but one of the side effects is some days you end up with fake nails in the car park.

A BLACK AND WHITE
PHOTOGRAPH OF 130 WHITE MEN

The earliest photo of the club we have is a black and white photo of 130 men stood in three lines, like an old school photograph, in front of a brick building with HOLBECK WORKING MEN'S CLUB written in beautiful, large, hand painted lettering on the front. The windows are arched – unstained but otherwise like small church windows. And every man is wearing a tie, most in waistcoats and all in jackets. There's the spit of Harold MacMillan in the back row, one of only a handful of moustaches, not a beard amongst them and the majority clean shaven.

Without the sign, it could be a number of historically important gatherings of white men in black and white photos that we are used to seeing. But there is something in the used nature of the clothing and a little tiredness around each of the faces that tells us that this is a group of working men, or at least not princes and officers and statesmen.

But still they were well enough connected to be able to reach out to Lady Ingram – she who lived in the big pile Temple Newsam in North Leeds – to borrow the money to build the club in the 1870s. The local school, and numerous roads still carry her name, but the club has no mention of her. Stand in the club car park now and you can still see one of the original arched windows amongst the numerous late 20th century extensions – a flat roof that gets repaired with almost Sisyphean regularity, and cement rendering which hides the original 19th century brick work (and that beautiful sign one would imagine).

But there is no mention of the aristocratic woman who bankrolled the operation. Perhaps understandably, because lending the money was the last thing a woman did in the club for nearly a hundred years. Working men's clubs took the first of those two words literally for a long time until society's inevitable progression stopped them.

The first paragraph of the club's friendly society constitution reads, 'The objects of the club are to afford its members the means of social intercourse, mutual helpfulness, mental and moral improvement and rational recreation,' which sounds pretty good to me.

Originally a place for education and self-growth, the club was a lecture hall and games room. Owned by the members, these clubs were gentle experiments in collectivism. A late Victorian understanding of the need for adult education, relaxation and non-work stimulation: culture.

Holbeck working men's club, like nearly all of them, grew up in an era of the temperance movement so the bar was not a focus in those first decades. Later, it became more important as a means to raise funds for the educational activity and social events.

There are still members that remember a fleet of coaches sat outside the club every August, ready to take hundreds away to Blackpool for the week. A trip afforded by the profits of the bar.

One can be too starry-eyed about a system that relied on the increasing alcoholism of working men to afford a leisure and cultural life for the families, but there is a sense of collective responsibility and action that runs through so much of how the club has behaved over the 150 years. As long as you're a man of course. And being white helped too. These are truths too.

Entertainment became increasingly important in the 20th century and HWMC became the try-out venue for the northern club circuit. Ernie Wise performed there with his father, and there were few acts that did well on the post-war club circuit who didn't pass through The Holbeck.

Members' wives were finally introduced in the 1950s, although membership in their own right would have to wait a few more decades.

It is the received wisdom that the industrial decline of the 1980s and the smoking ban of 2007, along with increases in alcohol duty, led to the downfall of this sort of club (and certain types of pub). It's undeniable that all these things will have had an impact. I'll also never get tired of blaming Thatcher for stuff.

But it is also true that, as glorious as much of its beginnings were and the dream of collective action shines out even now, clubs like this have a sense of exclusion right at the heart of their origin myth. It's not even that they were for working men. Or even white working men. They were, like all clubs, cliquey. The process of becoming a member was complicated, and reliant on being vouched for and supported by other members. What chance an Irishman perhaps? Let alone a person of colour. Or a single woman, even in the 80s.

And like all membership organisations that have no need to critique themselves or let strangers in, their hinterland grows shallower, and they become dominated by a small number of voices; and become known for a slight slither of their whole potential. In this instance, a pub that opened for two sessions on a Sunday.

In a community with many Muslims, and many non-drinkers, and many people who couldn't afford (or didn't want to) drink in a bar for hours on end, this was financial suicide. If you're a membership organisation and your members are dying faster than new members are arriving, then your fifth act is accelerating towards you.

The Holbeck was lucky in that a group of volunteers came and threw their weight behind the club's survival, but they did so often in the face of opposition; changes to membership rules, and what the club was for were often unpopular with the shrinking group of established members.

And so it was with our arrival. It's not that we want to stop the place being a pub on a Sunday, it's just that it has to be so much more than that if it's going to continue to be relevant to the whole community for years to come. And, despite the very obvious financial and political pressures that make these changes inevitable, I can well imagine how difficult it was – with its labyrinthine committee structures and restrictive membership policies – to try and make any change that might have seen the club ride those Thatcher-caused waves. The world in which the club made sense was changed profoundly and too often it refused to change with it.

An organisation that took seventy-five years to let women in the place was always going to find the changes that Slung Low brought with them hard to stomach. Every part of our community is now welcome to use the club and most of them use it for something other than Sunday drinking and bingo. And that's okay. No matter what anyone tells you.

But, that all said, at its heart it feels like Slung Low is coming home. Lending our energy to a place that for over 140 years has been a palace of 'social intercourse, mutual helpfulness, mental and moral improvement and rational recreation.' Too right. And we were about to take that mutual helpfulness to a whole new level. But first, we were going to have to close the bar. Again.

A POWER GRAB SHUT DOWN

The Coronavirus crisis hit in March of 2020.

The weekend before, as Covid had moved from something distinctly foreign and distant, to hand sanitiser shortages and fear, I had been down in Plymouth with the first public workshop of a new show to mark the 400th anniversary of the Mayflower's landing at the Theatre Royal there.

150 members of the public on stage for a weekend. I was not liking this. These groups are traditionally elderly, we knew we had a number of participants with low immune systems, thanks to excellent outreach in the disabled community. All rammed together on a stage, moving, touching.

On the way down on the long train journey from Yorkshire to Plymouth I'd tried to suggest to the theatre management they stop the workshop. It wasn't lost on me as I stepped off the train at Plymouth that, at its heart, the story of the Mayflower is the story of strangers arriving with a disease that will destroy a place called Plymouth. I mean, don't tempt the wrath of theatre gods, they love it when history rhymes.

My boss was not appreciating the metaphor, 'It'll blow over, you'll see, we'll be talking about something else in a month.'

I couldn't get the theatre management to shift on stopping the weekend activity. Resigning from the gig felt like a particularly cowardly way to demonstrate my leadership and duty of care. The other creatives were ringing saying they were no longer able to make it down to Plymouth, staff at the theatre started to get stressed about what risks they were being exposed to. It was unravelling as the news headlines spoke of an imminent lockdown.

Why were we pushing on with this? It was a potential case study of a spreader event in a vulnerable community: words I hadn't even heard of forty-eight hours ago which now I shouted into phones at unmoved theatre managers.

Someone took me to one side. 'It's about the insurance.'

'What is?'

'Why they won't stop the weekend. If they close before they're told to the insurance won't pay out.'

'Are you for real?'

'It's hundreds of people's jobs if they get this wrong.'

'I don't... If they get this wrong and this is the spreader event of the south.'

'I'm just saying...'

As this conversation was happening and as good men and women of The Theatre Royal Plymouth wrestled honestly with their responsibilities to various communities there was a horse race meeting with tens of thousands of people which had been contrived as safe. I'm still struck by the difference of care and attention that a few hundred people were given in Plymouth and the complete lack of any of that given to thousands of punters blithely bimbling to Cheltenham.

So there I was, in the weekend of panic in the South West with a hundred or so people about to arrive and spit all over each other in a workshop whilst the Government were warning that total lockdown was no more than a week away. And stopping the workshop seemed out of my authority. I wondered what the limit of my authority was. I found the Executive Producer.

'I can't cancel the workshop?'

'No sorry.'

'But I decide what we do here? How long for?'

'Well yes.'

'Great. Get them in – set them two metres apart in the biggest circle we can. We'll read the play and then send them home before lunch. No touching, no workshop. The event has not been cancelled but we get them out as quick as we can.'

She seemed as relieved as me. No one had wanted this damn thing to go ahead. The square had been circled.

And as I jumped on the last train to Leeds out of the south west that night the mood had changed. Fellow train passengers tense and scrunched up tight. I spoke to Joanna on the phone as the train meandered its way north. The vast majority of our members were elderly, many had COPD, or had only just stopped smoking. There are no windows in the bar or lounge area. It was a disaster waiting to happen. Shut the club early. Get her shut now.

We closed and then in a few days the Government announced that all pubs would shut.

But the few days early had cost us with the die-hards in the established membership.

On Monday morning there would be a series of voicemails left at the club in a couple of different, elderly but angry northern voices. 'You cheats! We knew you'd betray us as soon as you could. It's disgusting that you've shut our club. DISGUSTING!' And on they went.

I don't think these members understand how digital phones work or the joys of 1471. We laughed. It had become emblematic of our relationship with a small rump of established members, that even as we forwent the last income we would see for many a month in order to avoid an outbreak of deadly Covid in the membership, they had seen it as a power grab by us. Facing down the prospect of the bar being closed for a few months and being on the hook for the losses that would follow, I wasn't sure where they got the idea that we wanted even the power that we had already, let alone any more, but there was no reasoning with them. Matching the mood of the age, they had been betrayed. They wouldn't forget it.

LETTER TO OUR 200 NEIGHBOURS

With the bar shut and our normal activities temporarily outlawed in Lockdown 1, we set about thinking about the most useful thing we could do now. Our funders, especially the Arts Council of England, had got in touch almost immediately to confirm that they would be flexible and supportive – just survive through this and we'll work out what to do after. We were in the lucky position of having no worries about our mortgages – we'd be okay. Days before the word furlough passed Rishi's lips publicly, we'd got in touch with the bar staff to say we were good for their wages too. We'd sink or swim together.

It's easy to forget the sense of urgency in those first few lockdown days – a surreal sense that comes from living the same events as those in the news headlines: that doesn't happen very often, certainly not to a whole nation at once.

In those moments it is easier to have discussions about what is right to do, what the moral path forward is, when the everyday ceases.

It was clear in the moment that abandoning the club would be against everything we had said we were for. It was clear, even just in the houses immediately around the club, that there was need, people were worried. And we were in a position to help.

So, we wrote a letter to the 200 houses immediately around The Holbeck, a letter to our neighbours.

The Slung Low team are still here in the office at the club and we are currently healthy and full of energy. We have cars and a van. And you are our neighbours and if there is anything we can do for you in the coming weeks please do not hesitate to ask.

If you are isolating, or can't leave the house for other reasons please know that you can call on us to lend a hand.

Immediately people were in touch. Government schemes for the shielding and clinically vulnerable would kick in over the coming weeks but in those first moments all over the country it was these small moments of mutual aid that got people through.

Elderly neighbours who obediently locked themselves up in their homes but found themselves locked out of the supermarket delivery process that fell over in those first few days. Or those without internet access and the confidence to navigate the support systems that had been set up nationally. We did people's shopping, walked dogs, picked up prescriptions. Just a few a day. Mostly neighbours who, despite our best efforts the past year, we didn't know. Mostly people who, embarrassed, would say when they call, 'I don't normally need help but they say I'm not allowed to leave the house, I normally manage fine on my own.'

Word got out. First to the other voluntary organisations in Holbeck that we were willing to pitch in. We started driving for Holbeck Food Bank. We did a couple of weeks' shifts for the local meals on wheels. In the space of a couple of days we'd managed to create the portfolio of useful little tasks for other organisations in the area. Useful and kind.

INVITATION TO CARE

The club has been shut three weeks. I'm in the wood that Slung Low manage. Cliff Wood. Sixteen acres in the Holme Valley, of oaks, beech and silver birch. It's only about 400m of steep hill that runs about 1200m long. On the one long edge is a water works. Once a month it wafts the smell of toilet over the wood and on the other long edge the sleepy rail line that runs between Sheffield and Huddersfield. Once an hour a two-carriage old bone-rattler comes through, but you can stand in the middle of the wood and be lost in it.

We're building an outdoor classroom on the only flat bit of the wood at the top of the hill.

It's the first flush of lockdown, so the idea that an outdoor space will be particularly useful for the next two years is only just coming into focus, but it was something that we had been wanting to do anyway and all of a sudden I find myself with some time on my hands.

The bar is closed, and we've cancelled all the upcoming shows for three months, paying each visiting company the box office they might have expected from the gig. So even with the new delivery work we're still nowhere near as busy as we would be usually.

And more importantly in terms of blank calendars the year's big show, *This Land*, has just been postponed. *This Land* had been an overly ambitious community theatre project for the 400th anniversary of the landing of The Mayflower. A collaboration between the folk singer Seth Lakeman, playwright Nick Stimson, 150 UK Plymouthians and thirty-five members of the Wampanoag tribe. The Wampanoags had been the tribe on the beach when The Mayflower landed in 1620 – and royally screwed ever since.

In the first lockdown the Trump government was taking the tribe through the US courts to disprove their very existence which was quite the move, even for Trump.

With the 400th commemoration, in an effort to avoid the celebratory and ill-judged events of previous anniversaries, we had committed to ensuring that this time the story would include the Wampanoag's story and voice – their story.

In reality, this meant two years of trips to small community halls in Massachusetts to listen to members of the tribe and try to convince them of our good intent and usefulness. It hadn't been easy. There is a good deal of understandable anger in the community and often my arrival would give them a perfectly acceptable target for that anger.

But over the months we had stood in the rain and patiently soaked up as much of that anger as we could. With each visit, each workshop, each conversation we had earned some trust and proved our hearts, if not pure, then at least useful. And on the last visit we had settled upon a text that the tribe members had found pride and pleasure in, words they would perform in the show that was planned: a milestone I had feared would never be reached.

With Covid breaking, I was on the cusp of a rehearsal period that would see me race between the two Plymouths – UK and US – for nine weeks before bringing it all together on the main stage of the colossal Theatre Royal Plymouth. Doing anything like this sort of travel on a British regional theatre budget is not without its discomforts and pain, but the script was powerful, profound and entirely without precedent and in the Theatre Royal Plymouth I had found a brave and determined partner. I had my bag packed for the endeavour – the Wampanoag would speak and be heard. This was the work of 2020 and it was just about to start.

And then, even in that first week of lockdown, it became clear that a project that involved this much international travel for so many – let alone dealing with a story that is at its heart about white men taking a deadly virus to indigenous people by repeatedly visiting an indigenous community in a time of global pandemic – was never going to happen in 2020. And all of a sudden, the dance card was empty, the calendar deleted, and the year stretched ahead of me. Which is how I came to be standing on an old tree stump in Slung Low's wood on a Tuesday morning.

We had cleared a couple of trees from our site and would eventually have a bespoke canvas made and then stretched between seven trees with an ingenious system of ratchet straps and metal cabling. Taken all together it would create a magical, handsome, canvassed classroom. But for now, I was connecting each tree with twine and then planning to take a picture of it all from a drone so designer David Farley could turn the madness of string into an actionable design.

There I was, standing on a tree stump, surrounded by two dozen connected string lines, like a detective closing in on a serial killer and the phone rang.

'Hello, it's Jane from the City Council. Joanna said it would be best to talk to you. Do you have a moment?'

'Yes of course.' I don't think I know Jane but I'm always forgetting people so I always I assume I know them if they seem familiar and see where it gets me. Joanna was on a well-deserved, and long desired, week's holiday. Obviously she was spending it locked up in her flat in Leeds, but I was still pleased that she wasn't having work chats with the council.

'Do you have any capacity at the moment?'

I'm looking at a clearing of string and the drone on the floor that I will inevitably crash after this call. I can hardly maintain I am rushed off my feet.

'Of course. What do you need?'

'Could you take some of the social care referrals from the city's coronavirus helpline?'

'Yes.' Some words in that last sentence from Jane I didn't recognise.

'Could you take the whole ward?'

'Ward?' I sort of know what a ward is but still.

'Holbeck and Beeston.'

'Sure!' When in doubt a cheerful enthusiasm is my default. It occasionally has led to some adventures I'd rather have avoided, but in my experience, most of the time it's fine. In fact, most times most people leave you alone, happy with your general positivity. Can I come down to talk about becoming a theatre director? Can I send you my play? Can I have my nanna's birthday party in your pub? I'm asked these things a dozen times a week and I cheerfully agree to everything – sure! Email me a day, send me a date, post me a play – and nearly all of them you never hear from again. And those who do, well nearly all of them are fine. I've never regretted saying yes to directing a play and I've never said no to one and it's taken me all over the world. So when in doubt, when confused or when I don't really know what a social care referral in a ward is, I say yes.

'Yes!'

'Ah that's great Alan. We'll be in touch.'

And she was gone. Jane. It'll be at least a week before she calls again, I thought as I finished my string. The council are always floating ideas, and it takes them forever to do anything. A lovely lot but incapable of acting quickly. I'll tell the rest of the gang about it tomorrow, in case it comes up with the Councillors, I thought as I readied the drone. And by the time I had, inevitably, crashed said drone into the web of string I had mostly forgotten about it.

The first referral would arrive 10am that next morning. By the end of the year 2020 we would have done 8,188 referrals and every part of our company would have changed.

Before all that could happen, we had to work out how to action social care referrals.

THE FOODBANK IN HOLBECK

As soon as we'd closed the club for Covid, we had offered to drive for Holbeck Food Bank.

HFB has been going for years. Part of the Mosaic church, it was now run by a lovely woman called Hannah and an older couple called David and Barbara Hebden.

David was the dominant force. We already knew him from around the club, the church group and as treasurer of Holbeck Gala. He runs an incredibly slick operation. A store cupboard in the local community centre crammed full of food, connections with FareShare and Trussell Trust along with local wholesalers, regular donations from the church and a bank account full of money. It is the quiet, determined, regular part of voluntary social safety net which is so familiar to every ward in the country. People doing good things on their own for the best of reasons. Quietly.

With the elderly being told to stay at home, and so much of this work is done by the retired, our brand-new enthusiasm was well timed.

David started sending the referral forms through to me and we would go to his store, pick up the food he and Barbara had packed into bags and deliver it to the address.

To get a parcel from HFB you needed to be referred by one of the services David recognised; a local church, probation, social care something like that. Carefully selected food in three bags would then be assigned you and delivered. In those first weeks maybe ten to fifteen referrals would meet the criteria.

HFB wouldn't allow certain individuals to receive any more food. For example, if you had had more than three parcels within six months. That was as many as you could have from HFB. And you had to be referred to by one of these services, which themselves had their own selection criteria. At HFB and other organisations there was tension around sex workers and whether they 'qualified' for support given the nature of their work.

In short time this led to some discussion at Slung Low. We definitely didn't want David and Barbara, or their normal volunteer drivers who we knew to be in the at-risk category, to start delivering again. We knew we were useful in taking on that more risky part of the operation.

It was also true that access to HFB's food store was on occasion very useful. If we were short, we would grab a few extra bags when we were picking up their deliveries. It really made the difference some days.

Equally, we had committed to playing our part during Covid for entirely moral reasons; despite the financial cost, personal risk and hard bloody work that it entailed. Being driven by moral imperative meant that supporting a system that we didn't agree with hardly made sense.

And yet we knew that this would all be over one day, we'd go back to doing what we did and falling out with people – people who had been quietly getting on with the hard work when we were making shows for the Royal Shakespeare Company and poncing about in Singapore making theatre – that didn't seem particularly moral either.

The sex worker issue was easy enough. Contacting the local charities that support sex workers (we're blessed with some blindingly brilliant ones in Holbeck at Basis Yorkshire and the Joanna Project) and explaining that we would take any and all referrals from them would take the pressure out of that moment.

But then there was the issue of 'three parcels and out'. I'd try talking to David.

I explained that there isn't enough food in these parcels to last a family a week, let alone the six weeks that the no-more-than-three-parcels-per-six-month rule would require.

He explained it was to stop people getting addicted to food parcels.

We went back and forth. It wasn't an easy conversation.

Delivering food to people tests your humanity. You see cruelty. You see despair. You see people taking the piss out of your service. And you might see all of that in one delivery. Or every delivery for a day. For a week. And this couple had, almost on their own, done this work for years. Quietly. Unheralded. Their humanity had been tested. Over and over. And yet here they still were.

And here I was. A few weeks in to giving it a go. Telling them the rules by which we would participate. And yet we couldn't carry on supporting the system we know we didn't agree with.

'Just send the referrals you are going to reject and we'll deliver to them using food that isn't yours. That way everything can stay the same.'

It wasn't an easy conversation. He wasn't impressed. He left. We were unresolved.

And then a few weeks later he popped into the club again.

'God has spoken to me Alan and he's told me that we must deliver more than three parcels to families. Whilst the Covid crisis is going on.'

God is nearer the surface than you'd expect in Holbeck. He comes up a lot. As someone without faith I found it surprising at first, then a little funny, then it started to make sense.

No one is an atheist in a fox hole. And whilst Holbeck isn't at war, it nonetheless is a painful and violent place at times. Often. Like so many overlooked parts of our nation it has within it so much that is upsetting. Much that is cruel.

I think you can understand this without disrespecting our neighbours. You can know this whilst understanding the glory of the place too.

And so it doesn't surprise me that those who deal with the day-to-day of Holbeck find God, whichever one they recognise, so often on their shoulders. It's rare for him to be so clear on an issue though. Even rarer to find that he and I were of one mind on an issue.

Still, you take the wins where you can and until the end of the year 2020, we would continue to deliver HFB's referrals.

I would grow to become incredibly fond of David and Barbara, despite or even maybe because of David's inability to hide any grumpiness he felt at the people around him not doing as they were told. I don't agree with them on everything and they quite rightly don't give a shit about that.

They, and the thousands like them, are the volunteers who long before anyone had heard of Covid got on with the thankless, tiring job of trying to sustain a system that was capable of repairing some of the damage that our society unthinkingly causes. It was this system that so many of us who stepped into the Covid breach got to grab hold of and shake and repurpose and drive forward.

It wasn't until long after those initial moments of crisis that I thought about how hard it must have been to create and sustain that system in the first place. Those who did that were quiet, everyday heroes.

YOU'VE GOT TO HAVE A SYSTEM

We're having a team meeting about this social care referral thing that happened yesterday.

'So, people ring the council helpline?'

'Yep.'

'And then the council send their details to us?'

'Yep. In a spreadsheet.'

'And we do what they need?'

'Yeah.'

'With what?'

We'd been given £5,000 by the council immediately to support operations. Which was nice but was a different level of funding than we were used to operating on – a cabaret might cost that much here at the club. Here we are working in theatre, complaining, with some justification, that we're badly funded when we were being asked to service the city's Coronavirus helpline for the ward for five grand.

'How long for?' asks Joanna. That week off hasn't survived the news that we run a social care service, so she's back in.

'I don't know. They're saying three months.'

The first few referrals were a mix of things. Lots of people just checking in, but not actually needing anything yet. The delivery services for supermarkets had just crashed with the news of a lockdown and there was a general panic about toilet paper across the nation. No one really knew what they were doing.

And then the referrals started to come in. Eric, a lonely, lovely old man who was scared of leaving the house and whose internet kept breaking. Hannah, who had four kids and very precise food requirements that mostly revolved around frozen chips. Simon who couldn't get his bins out to the street. Mums whose cleaning work had dried up and found themselves smashed about by the benefits system. The elderly and shielding who daren't go to the chemists for their prescriptions.

The first few days it was okay to fight hand to hand: just doing each referral as a separate piece of work. Fetch a bag of shopping from One Stop Shop and deliver to Brian. Then fetch a prescription and drop off with Muriel. And so on. But as we criss-crossed back and forth to the same parts of town and the number of referrals kept increasing it became clear at the end of the first week that we needed a system.

I was only a couple of months out of the short commissioning course at Royal Military Academy Sandhurst. I'm a Reservist in the Royal Engineers and mercifully the course at Sandhurst is full of training that is incredibly useful if you need to bring some form of control to an inefficient problem – and by god this was an inefficient problem. The referrals often led chaotic lives. The council would often miss out vital information, like where the food needed delivering to or a phone number. The food was coming either from irregular private donation or The Real Junk Food Project which redistributed food no longer needed by the supply chain, the actual definition of inefficiency. The volunteers, newly directed to us by Claire, our wonderful handler from the Voluntary Action Leeds scheme, were brilliant but they too were often juggling many demands and trying to cope with a global pandemic and do the right thing at the same time.

This was a civic problem that needed a solution rooted in mutual aid. But for that to work the core of the machine had to be rigid, the organised engine that would give the other parts the slack it needed to work.

Reinventing models of doing things had always been at the heart of what Slung Low does; whether it's water-borne theatre shows on floating fiery platforms or managing a social club, the game had always been to identify the problem and then build a formation for the company to achieve it. Regular radical change was in our DNA: we knew how to change shape, we just needed to know what our new shape was going to be.

It became immediately clear that the biggest danger was someone not getting their food, someone going hungry. So we put in a double system to check: whiteboards and treasury cards alongside Excel spreadsheets to ensure that not only would each task get done but it could also be easily checked that it was done. And recorded: we had to be sure, even days after, that each and every task had been done.

This was the focus – the bit that could go wrong without full concentration – so it was moved up into our big performance space: the 250 seater cabaret event room which once had the likes of Ernie Wise perform on it, and only last year saw Divina De Campo belt out Whitey Houston numbers. Now it was a room full of white boards and laptops and each and every job was written up, checked, dispatched and recorded.

The food sorting and bagging went downstairs in the main bar, boxes of blueberries and loaves of bread lined up on the covered pool table: it allowed easy access from the car park and the volunteers who couldn't deliver to usefully pack bags whilst social distancing.

And the volunteer management itself was separated off. Sally was still holed up in Sheffield and organising the befriending calls – a huge part of what we did for the first four months – could be done safely from home.

Quickly we got to fifty referrals a week and the system held up. The volunteers kept coming and the food kept flowing. Matt would race around the city in the company van, picking up whatever was offered to us, Joanna would keep the volunteers scheduled and returning data to the council on each and every delivery and Sally would ensure the lonely were called by those who found themselves at home with time on their hands and the desire to help.

And I would stand in the middle and make sure, best that I could, that need met resource, effort met impact. We committed to speaking to every referral. We'd call and reassure those on the other end of the line that we were on our way today. Every referral would be met within twenty-four hours, that was our promise.

And, notwithstanding the odd confusion or moment, we did. And that's how it worked for the first few months of the Covid crisis, until the pub reopened, and the weekly numbers crept above 200.

STRANGERS IN THE ATTIC

Not every call was a problem that could be fixed. Some people needed much more help than we could ever manage to give.

One woman rang day after day. She was certain that people were trying to dig through the walls from the house next door. She'd cry and put the phone down. We started reporting it up the chain into whoever we could find in the council: there was no return signal there. She would ring again. Each time in more and more emotional pain.

She'd ask for unusual food, 'some custard would make me feel better', we'd find some custard and send it round. The next day she'd be back on the line – 'the bastards are trying to come in through the cellar. If they come in here, I'll kill them, I'LL KILL THEM.'

I finally managed to get hold of adult mental health.

A tired and pissed-off voice answered. I explained the situation.

'Call the police.'

'What?'

'Call the police. She's threatened others. She's a danger, call the police.'

'She isn't a danger, she's just broken. Can we do something?'

'You can call the police.'

'Oh, this is ridiculous there must be something better than criminalising her.'

The sigh from the adult mental health man at the end of the phone suggested that I didn't know what I was talking about.

I put the phone down. They were right. I was a theatre director with some bags of food.

The woman called back – this time they were in the attic space, coming for her.

I urged her to ring the police. She did. They attended. Found nothing. Left her to it. Over and over, we would urge her to call the police. Because there was nothing else to do apparently. This is what we did when a woman thought there were men burrowing under their house coming for them and she armed herself in readiness with her kitchen knife – call the police. This went on for weeks. The police would arrive, would leave. What else were they meant to do?

It snapped me.

And then one day the phone rings. It's her. Tired and pissed off I answer.

'They're still there,' she whispers, 'waiting in the attic. They're going to get me when I fall asleep.'

'I'm coming over.' This whole time, weeks and weeks of this, her house had only ever been 400 metres away. I'm in the car, racing around the moor and to the address I know off by heart.

BANG BANG. 'Let me in Susan, it's Alan.'

'They're upstairs. They're upstairs!'

'Right let's be having you, you bastards!' and I'm up the stairs, a ball of frustration and adrenaline.

The stairs – on both floors up to the attic conversion – are lined by piles of boxes and plastic bags full of random objects, a wall of soap powder, a dozen suitcases there – chaos. Chaos that I trip over as I manage to fall up two flights of stairs, like a competitor in one of those strange gameshows made in Japan you see on late night telly.

I finally make it into the attic, burst through the door, enraged. There is, of course, no one there.

'They've smashed through the wall!' she shouts from downstairs.

They haven't. The walls are intact.

I stand in the attic and I have no idea what to do next. I knew they wouldn't be here but hadn't thought what would come next.

I sit on the floor and get my breathing back to non-panting levels. I'm out of solutions. This first two months had been nothing but problem solving and determined logistics and here I am, sat amongst the physical manifestations of a woman's mental breakdown, and none of that will work.

What am I doing?

I compose myself and go down the stairs. Falling back over all the random piles once again.

I sit her down. We have a talk. I do my best. I look her in the eye and tell her that she can ring whenever she needs, we'll always answer, we'll always deliver what we have but she needs to go and see her doctor and keep going until she gets help.

It doesn't go in – even as I'm leaving, she's telling me they're back in the attic.

I drive back to the club.

GIVE US YOUR FOOD

These first few weeks we were left more or less to our own devices. Every week we would be emailed yet another spreadsheet with all the details of our volunteers and various council staff members would ring from outposts in the city with 'I've got thirty food bags, have you got any nappies?' or 'Can you make use of 1000 avocados?' We continued to hack away at the referral list – dispatching volunteers with whatever we'd managed to get a hold of from an increasingly large network of small local charities.

We'd been sent letters from the city council's Chief Exec explaining that we were volunteers, we were running a food hub and were not to be stopped by any travel restrictions or police roadblocks that were all the rumour for the first months. I put my name on one, laminated it and stuck it the windscreen of my car feeling like a member of the underground resistance, as people moaned for hours on the internet about their Boris bimble only being an hour.

The five grand the City Council gave us wasn't going to last, so we started to look around for alternative supplies of food. We got it from all sorts of places, relying on The Real Junk Food project. The local churches rallied round too, we raided the Holbeck Food Bank store on the days we ran out and for a while took up the excess from local cash and carries.

One day when were out of milk and feeling the pinch we sent Matt to the local Co-op.

'Put a high-visibility jacket on, find the manager, explain we're a food bank down the hill and we need milk and bread.'

'Will they just give me it?'

'It's got to be worth a shot.'

It was and they did. And, until a regional manager found out and asked why we weren't going through their corporate charitable given scheme, they gave us bread and milk at least once a week for months.

Slung Low isn't a charity. For lots of reasons. For starters, look at the political pressure the government are putting on charities not to campaign against the causes of the social injustice they spend their time and money trying to fix. Or the inequalities that are baked into who we ask to sit on the boards of our cultural charities. And the wrong-headed idea that real change can happen if you leave final authority in the hands of people who, by definition, have done very well out of the current system.

But in large part it's because I don't want to work for other people. Slung Low, if it has achieved anything, has achieved it because of the work and commitment and sacrifice and talent of my friends. And I don't want to have to hand over that authority or responsibility to a committee of the great and good.

If we'd been a charity, we would never have been allowed to pivot so quickly and so fully to serving the people of Holbeck and Beeston. Our charitable aims would not have matched our current activity – the board would have been duty and legally bound to rein us in. The lack of a board makes us rare, but not quite unique, in publicly funded theatre companies.

All of which had served us very well until we started trying to pry food out of corporate systems which didn't have room for the slightly more nuanced idea that this wasn't some sort of complicated scam.

Fortunately, we had Adam Smith at The Real Junk Food Project, our army of supporters online, and the silver tongue of our Matt when things got really desperate.

So it drove along those first few months. We'd get names and numbers from the council on a spreadsheet – I'd ring them, have a chat, see what they needed and nine times out of ten sent them some bags of fresh food.

We were starting to get into a rhythm and two thirds of the way through that first three months I thought we might make it to the end in one piece.

CALL ME, TEXT ME,
MISSED CALL ME

And then we got a note from the council. A new rule. A client can only refer through the system a total of four times.

I emailed our city council handler, a lovely man, a reassigned lawyer called Jabbar. What was all this about only four times, Jabbar?

The council were concerned about people becoming addicted to food parcels.

A Labour city council. Worried about addiction to food parcels. What in the name of all that is puritan and snotty was this nonsense now?

I put on my Hulk suit and set to work firing emails to all and sundry promising resistance.

It was not long before the phone rang. Ward Councillor.

'Alan, I saw your note about the idea of becoming addicted to food parcels.'

'You can't become addicted to food, it's an obscene political philosophy...'

'I agree.'

'...It's Victorian moralising of the worst kind and fails to understand the inherent unfairness and cruelty of both the current benefits system and the zero-hour contract economy that so much of our community relies upon. An economy, I might add, that has been completely destroyed by Covid.'

'Yes, I agree.'

'You do?'

'Yes, that's what I was ringing to say.'

'Oh sorry, I got on a bit of a roll there, probably didn't need to tell a Labour councillor for South Leeds all that.'

'No.'

'Right. Sorry about that.'

'You can rely on our support.' And then they were off.

We didn't need the encouragement, but it never hurts, and we used it to galvanise ourselves to circumvent this new rule.

'Okay Helen, this is your third referral.'

'Yeah, things are really tough and my money has been delayed.'

'We quite understand, not a problem. It's just if you ring the council again then you won't be able to get another parcel.'

'I need the food, I'm not taking the piss with this...'

'I know. Helen, I know. So don't ring the council again. Ring the number I've called you on and just let us know what you need.'

'This number?'

'Yep. My phone, ring that and not the council understand?'

'Got it.'

It took about a month to move all the existing referrals from calling the city helpline to our new line. New people could still ring the council line for help and their referral would be put through to us – but everybody already in the system would now ring us direct. It confirmed our commitment to doing what was necessary to help our neighbours. It removed the unpleasant moralising tone of some of the referrals which would reach us through the council portal. And most importantly, it secured in the minds of our community this supply of food. It kept our promise, that no one would go hungry during the Coronavirus crisis in Holbeck and Beeston. This was our new promise.

We still committed to answering any referral the council sent us. They sent maybe six a week, but the vast majority of our weekly 250 weekly referrals would come from partners and people directly requesting help.

We'd won the values battle. If we were going to do this, we were going to do it our way, with our moral code. But there was a cost. The relationship was now directly with the community, the council had no reason to continue to support the venture financially. We would survive without their money, but we were aware of what we had done. And so were the council.

'You can't say you're going to feed the world and then have us pay for it.'

'We're not feeding the world and you're only paying 20% of what it's costing.'

Mercifully, calmer heads prevailed. Wiser voices who reframed this as a wonderful, modern collaboration between many partners – a test case of the city council letting go of power. And as a result, the city council kept their funding in place.

And we had a new way of talking about what we were doing – the language kindly given by colleagues who had been at this a lot longer than us – a non-means tested, self-referral food bank.

'What does that mean?'

'If anyone asks for food, we give it.'

'Got it.'

THE OTHER ADAM SMITH

It was clear that we needed far more food than we could scrounge from the contacts at the council. And if we were buying all the food we were being asked for at market value, we wouldn't last long. For large parts of the year our main effort was finding the solution to the problem of a reliable, affordable supply of food.

There are few genuine radicals in the world. The good news for us is that Leeds has one.

Adam Smith is South Leeds born and bred. He's talked openly about his past. The substance abuse, expulsion from school, being found dead in a car – his self-described 'lost years'. Those are his stories to tell, not mine. But in understanding that his story contains some of those experiences, you come to realise that his activism, and extraordinary drive, energy and determination come from a place of empathy – of lived experience – and not of missionary zeal.

He was at the forefront of the Pay What You Feel culture with his cafés which have spread all over the world, transforming communities' relationship to food and the market.

His The Real Junk Food Project is a sprawling, brilliant, energetic, often chaotic project that engages with the huge, industrial levels of waste. There are warehouses all over the country, full of food and accelerating towards the moment when to dispose of them is more costly than any price they can reach in the market.

This is plannable when you are talking about old airport hangars of tins and dried goods but an altogether more frenetic situation when you start to involve bread, chilled food and the poisoned chalice that is milk. One minute a vital household staple, an expiry date ticks by and you're all of sudden staring at gallons of costly waste to be disposed of.

And this waste is built into the system, not an occasional accident that needs to be mitigated, but a daily result of a system that has reduced food cost to so little in bulk that it can afford to have this level of waste priced in.

A system that throws away this food despite knowing there are hungry mouths in every community they operate in – but those people have no part to play in their business plan. And, most importantly for Adam, a system that thinks nothing of the environmental impact of all this excess and waste, even as their corporate PR speaks of responsible action.

It is in this world Adam operates. With an almost savant-like understanding of supply chains, the difference between best before and expiry dates and applying the creativity of his chef training, The Real Junk Food Project looks to save the value contained within this waste. Whether it be in regular deliveries to schools, food banks, churches or the Freegan boxes that people can sign up to on The Real Junk Food app, they were at the vanguard of social food and political action long before Covid hit.

Adam is at heart an environmental campaigner. As he said on a podcast he did for us in the middle of the third lockdown, 'poverty is a political problem, food waste is an environmental one.' Food waste is not the opportunity to solve the political problem with free food but a universal issue that, along with other polluting practices, will see the destruction of the planet. Adam is dealing with a different scale of problem than we are: we're trying to feed our neighbours; he's trying to save the world.

And he has never been convinced that food banks are part of the solution. 'They sustain the problem, they don't fix the root issues in the system and they have judgement built in.' He bridles at people's suggestion that he 'gives food to poor people'. He doesn't. He's trying to stop food waste. He's trying to save the world. And he's doing it one articulated lorry of food waste at a time. It is extraordinary. It is working. He is changing the patterns and habits of tens of thousands of people with his operation. His Kindness Warehouse was our single most reliable partner throughout the whole Covid affair – the difference between success and failure every day.

One day very early on in the crisis my phone rang.

'Hi, it's Adam Smith, one of my board has rung saying Alan Lane needs help. What do you need?'

I explained we'd taken on answering the social care referrals, which meant sourcing food at scale, which we didn't really know how to do. He invited our van down to the warehouse to take whatever we wanted that afternoon, something he would reiterate every day for over a year.

There would be times when a lorry pulled up outside the club with half a dozen pallets full of everything from noodles to Nando's hot sauce, hot cross buns to tons of blueberries. It was extraordinary, the things and the amounts that Adam would deliver. A hundred bags of popcorn, each one as tall as me; several hundred bottles of alcohol-free gin. A transit van full of Marks and Spencer chocolate one time. Everyone in Holbeck pigging out on high quality easter eggs in June for a week.

And then there were the burgers.

In the first lockdown the world didn't quite work properly. It was hard to hire a van. Drivers would disappear from shifts because of symptoms or family isolating. The business of getting things from A to B was much more difficult. And even more so if your operations hadn't actually existed in the times before.

On St George's day my phone rings,

'Alan, it's Adam, have you got a van and a driver?'

I looked at the board, we didn't have many referrals in. I looked around, we also didn't have any drivers.

'It's a bit tight here today mate.'

'I don't ask if I'm not desperate.' Fair enough, he didn't.

'Okay pal, I'm on my way.'

I shout to the room that I was on my way to help Adam Smith and I wouldn't be too long. I get to his warehouse, stop the van. A forklift immediately pulls up and loads one pallet of boxes onto the van. You can just about get two pallets into our transit if you're a very good forklift drive and sure enough this lad is back with another one and just manages to slide it in. And then Adam appears.

'These are Burger King vegan burgers. Frozen. We've no more space for them here. I've got dozens of pallets' worth.'

'Okay,' I say, wondering where I'm taking them.

'In each box is one hundred burgers. There's sixty boxes on each pallet.'

'Okay.' I hope it's not that school in Seacroft, it's a bugger to get the van through the gates.

'If you've got another van, I've got another two pallets for you.'

'Sure, I'll call Matt, we'll bring the church's van.'

'Brilliant, owe you one.'

'Not at all, just paying you one back for once. Adam, where are these going?'

'What do you mean?'

'Where are these being delivered?'

'Wherever you want. They're yours.'

And off he swooshed as the other two pallets of vegan Burger King burgers arrived.

I now had several thousand frozen burgers to get rid of.

Mercifully they were halal which makes the job a tiny bit easier. Or at least increases the number of people you can offer them to.

Ruth and Joanna in the office hit the phones whilst we race two vans of slowly defrosting burgers around the city. An extraordinary example of the whole ridiculous situation that our food system relies on. Stick this under a grill for five minutes and slap it in a bun with some lettuce and mayonnaise and these burgers were worth £3. They were delicious. There's nothing wrong with them. But if they were still in the van come 6pm that night it was going to be a very expensive operation to get rid of them. They needed to get to freezers and fast.

Every school, foodbank, church we knew was getting a call as Matt and I bombed about the city. The deal was you had to take at least a box, we didn't have the time (nor the food hygiene situation) to split boxes. School kitchen managers were rationalising freezer space, soup kitchens reorganising menus as the city was awash with Burger King vegan burgers.

And at 5pm we returned to the club, exhausted, having given away tens of thousands of burgers to anyone (literally anyone) who would have them. Sweaty, tired and broken, Joanna met us in the car park.

'How did you do?'

We opened the first van.

'It's empty, that is brilliant! How many burgers is that?'

'12,000 I think, maybe a few more, I've lost the list.'

I opened the second van.

'Oh shit.'

'Yep.'

'How many is there?'

'Sixty boxes maybe.'

'What happened?'

'We filled every freezer we went to, we couldn't fit any more. We'll have to skip them. We can't let Adam know, he'll go nuts.'

I was beat. We'd been at it all day and I was ready for my bed. Joanna on the other hand had other ideas.

'We're getting rid of them. Come on, get the van started.'

And so that is how, on St George's Day 2020, Matt, Joanna, Ruth Saxton and myself spent two hours walking behind a slowly crawling van with the doors open shouting, 'FREE BURGER KING BURGERS!'

Word spread. People came running out of their houses, called friends, cars raced round the estate to find us. We gave away the final 6000 burgers to absolutely anyone who wanted them.

And, before any of them defrosted, they were gone.

For months after, until another one of our adventures topped it in the local imagination, there were people who would see us and wave smiling shouting 'burgers!' It wasn't the only time we would find ourselves with preposterous amounts of wholesale food, incredibly valuable yesterday, now surplus to requirements: but we would get better at finding homes for it, apps for food waste sprung up, networks were created.

It was only in those first few Wild West months that there was a need for driving the streets tossing boxes of frozen burgers to strangers. But there was a thrill to it, despite it being hard work. And a usefulness that was immediate and kind and galvanising.

There are few real-life radicals alive today. We are lucky that Adam Smith is one and he is our friend. Because we would have been lost without him and his The Real Junk Food Project.

As I write, there are at least 100 Burger King Vegan Burgers in my freezer at home. No matter how many I eat the number never seems to get smaller.

BE USEFUL, BE KIND

There are three clear values that Slung Low operates by.
Be useful.
Be kind.
Everyone gets what they want, but no one else gets to stop others getting what they want.

When we moved into the club it was that final 'but no one else gets to stop others getting what they want' that led to the most difficult conversations and allowed the most transformation.

And so it was with the foodbank. Our decision to become a non-means tested self-referral food bank meant that whoever asked for food would receive it. The authorities weren't all happy but the response from our own community was the most surprising. The idea of a feckless poor, sitting watching their flat screen with their half dozen children spawned to secure their council house, is a myth. A corruption of the reality that Capitalism requires parts of society to be on poorly paid zero-hour contract work, propped up by a moralising benefits system, that forces people to live in a poverty we're collectively content to allow, as long as we don't look too closely.

And one of the revelations that was most surprising in this whole affair is that nowhere is this myth most passionately felt than in the communities with the most food parcel need.

Little has shocked me more during this process than when we cannot raise anyone in a house and we ask the neighbours to take it in for them and they refuse. 'They don't deserve it.'

BEER GARDENS IN CAR PARKS

Toward the middle of the year the Government announced that you could once again open pubs, with rules around sitting outside and in groups of no more than six, plus a whole host of other regulations that seemed so alien when they were first declared.

The first day of re-opening the bar arrived. We had no idea how many members would turn up. We hadn't done any marketing beyond the members, because our capacity was so small with Covid rules. My main worry was that we wouldn't have room for everyone.

Mercifully it was a glorious day, which meant we could keep everyone outside where it was at least a little easier to manage things. A little.

Sunday mornings and dinner time, it's mostly men in their seventies who come to talk to each other. There are a few families, but it is mostly dominoes time. And these men, many of whom had been members long before I was born, could not understand why they could not sit with their friends six to a table.

'It's two households a table, one of you is going to have to move.'

'He's my brother.'

'That's not what household means.'

'This is ridiculous.'

'Please let me take your temperature!'

And so it went on. You'd turn your back and they'd move their chair. The bar staff got tired of asking them to move it back. The mood soured.

We had put up fencing and bunting in order to mark out space but as the tension rose and the beer was drunk and the sun beat down, they started to look a lot like pens.

Pens that no one had any intention of staying in.

There was aimless chat from the members about human rights and more aimed chat about how much I was enjoying this. I was fast running out of patience with the handful that were intent on starting a row and painfully aware that the others were watching, seeing what the response would be.

We weren't even busy yet. They weren't even drunk yet.

I put on my big boy voice. 'Sit down in your chair or we'll stop serving you. Do you understand that this is your last warning?' I was losing here.

'I'm not stopping here, it's bullying,' said the prime troublemaker, who but five minutes ago had been shouting in Joanna's face about how horrible she was. A man in his late seventies, all red and furious that he couldn't sit next to his friend.

And off he toddled with his friend, to the car parked on the road by the side of the club. The others started up now, furious that their friend had been driven out. 'Here it comes – he's like a prison guard!' they exclaimed in chorus.

And then out of the corner of my eye I saw the one of the old boys who had just left. He'd reached the step up to the pavement next to his car and managed to get both feet up on the kerb but not the weight over his toes. Arms came flying out, waving around. He was tottering. Slowly, very slowly, like a giant pine, falling backwards.

I ran as fast as I've ever moved. Over the twenty-five metres between me and the road and just in time, by the slightest of margins got my hand to his back and uprighted him.

A moment's pause.

'Thanks.'

'It's okay.'

'See you next week.'

'Yep. You okay?'

'I've only had a couple of drinks.'

'That wasn't... okay. Safe home.'

As I returned to the tables, a chorus of 'It's ridiculous!' started up again. It was going to be a long summer of trying to get old men to do what was in their best interests. They'd win in the end.

Their capacity for self-harm was genuine. It would always trump my determination because in the end they were just much more certain than I was. They really did think that it was all unnecessary and made up to humiliate them.

HOLY JESTERS

There is a thriving Christian community in the ward. Or rather there are a number of thriving Christian communities. And in one way or another they underpin so much of what happens in the area.

There aren't many meetings in Holbeck, no matter whether they start out about the local gala or improvements to housing, that don't soon become about sex workers.

The Neighbourhood Plan (a bit like a Parish Council) and the club's Committee are powered by the members of the elderly Christian fellowship group who, now operating as a leaderless group, broke from the church a few years back. This group, made up of retired and experienced men (and often their wives) sit across nearly all the official activity in the ward and throw energy and determination into the campaign against the Managed Approach (which made sex work legal in the area) that colours so much of civic society in the area.

But there is also a younger, less official, more progressive group of people moved by the spirit of a Christian God in Holbeck. Whether it be the brilliant marauding charity Kidz Klub or the quietly kind St Luke Cares, or any of a number of others, there are more than a dozen leaders gently getting on with the business of changing lives in whatever way they can.

Always reliable, kind and useful, although with a tendency to be dominated or shouted down by the sort of loud, mature voice that fill the civic roles, these younger leaders became key supporters as our morale kept smashing against those who found the idea of food banks either offensive or unnecessary.

There are two in particular, Jackson and Matt who regularly do the rounds, walking the streets seeking people out. One day I heard music and, looking out the office to see what was going on, saw a mobility scooter decked out like a pirate ship being driven by Jackson in a Captain Jack Sparrow costume. As it drew nearer, I could clearly make out the theme tune to *Pirates of the Caribbean*.

'What are you doing?'

'Spreading a little joy in this terrible lockdown,' Jackson answered, throwing me a Curly Wurly.

They would often walk into the club, perhaps decked out in a bright pink wig and sequinned rainbow jacket and ask the volunteers if anyone had a sore right knee, or painful shoulder.

'God has told me that I will find a shoulder in pain here and I should heal it.'

It took a little while to get used to, but it soon became clear that they were of good faith in a town in short supply.

They would dress up, make noise, check in on people and hand out chocolate. Like a faith filled walking pantomime or –

'You're Friar Tuck!'

'What?'

'I've just realised – this schtick – it's Friar Tuck. Larger than life, handing out chocolate with a bit of faith healing on the side.'

'I like that,' they exclaimed before pushing off on a set of scooters they'd borrowed for the day.

They were kindly, well-meaning jesters. Putting their head above the parapet in a place where few were willing to stand out, look different, be weird. Be other. For all that their Christian belief ran through their antics they reminded me so much of theatre people – gently defiant, a kindness to their noise and nonsense – more like strolling players of old than any church I recognised from my Roman Catholic upbringing. And all the better for it.

They would often pray for Matt's back or my knees – both knackered from endlessly hoiking bags of spuds and tins of beans out of vans.

And then they'd always return a few days later,

'Do your knees still hurt?'

'No, all good.'

'Excellent! You've been healed.'

'Yes, it doesn't hurt any more. Thank you.'

I didn't have the heart to tell them I was chewing a dozen ibuprofen a day and I could barely feel my face, let alone my knees. But I also didn't want to tell them. I know more than anyone that any type of leadership even, or especially, the type that sees you dress up as a pirate and drive around the neighbourhood in a borrowed mobility scooter requires momentum; momentum built by enough of those exchanges just gently going your way.

It was hard holding the ground sometimes – fights with the council, wrestling with FareShare, members wanting the foodbank out of the club – it was all a bit much some days as we strove to keep the supply of food flowing and the volunteers in good spirits. And then these wild men would arrive – demonstrably on our side, willing us on, dressed as ballerinas or pirates or whatever it was today. They were good people in a tough world. We needed Jackson and Matt. Just as much as they needed my knees to be fixed.

LADYLIKE WORK PLACE

Despite all the stresses and arguments about the reopening rules, some of the members could not wait to return. They'd spent their adult lives sitting in this bar every Sunday evening with the same people – months away had been difficult for them.

We could barely fit two dozen downstairs according to the social distancing rules, so we decided to move the seating upstairs into the event room. In the day-time members could sit outside at distanced tables in the car park, and in the evening they could move upstairs into the big room. All table service, like the old days, but this meant more staff on for less customers.

But at least there would be room for everyone and plenty of space for bingo, around which the Sundays revolved. It meant moving the foodbank into the two small rooms downstairs – the lounge and the snooker room – but this way everybody could get what they wanted with just a little effort on our part.

It went well enough for a couple of weeks. The numbers were down, as many of the older group stayed away and we certainly didn't make any money. But with many members back after months of isolation, there was a joy around the place after months of silence. As difficult as it was, there was also a real sense that this is what social clubs are for: people who had been isolated for months back together again in each other's company, enjoying the simple collective things in life.

And then President Terry called a meeting of the Club Committee.

He was unhappy that the fences outside made it look like people were in pens. He wasn't wrong. There was no softening the aesthetic with bunting and decorations (which we'd tried). Fundamentally we had created pens. We couldn't get the men who arrived Sunday morning to abide by the rules – no more than two households to a table – without a physical barrier. There wasn't anything I could do, I explained. Pubs had been caught not obeying the rules and fined large amounts of money. The outside seating was clear for all to see from the road, police often passed by, we couldn't risk so bold a breach of rules governing pubs: President Terry wouldn't want to risk a fine or even worse closure? What does he suggest I do? He ignored me and pushed onto what he was really vexed about.

'It doesn't work with us upstairs,' President Terry announced.

'It's the only way we can fit everyone in.'

'It's not right, the girls don't look ladylike when they have to carry drinks upstairs.'

I was gobsmacked. It had been so much work to get everything ready to open the pub again on Sundays and fit the foodbank into the small rooms downstairs. We were losing more money opening than if we had stayed closed. The bar staff didn't like coming in because none of the members would obey social distancing rules. We'd overcome so many problems and put in so much work to get the place back open. And now this nonsense about ladylike bar staff.

'They're professionals grown adults, it's not acceptable to refer to them as ladylike.' Joanna was, like the Forlorn Hope, charging President Terry. It was forlorn because he had already retreated into his selective deafness.

'We're moving back downstairs,' President Terry insisted.

I looked around at the rest of the committee. The majority who had come to the meeting didn't trust the members to obey the distancing rules enough to risk their own health by coming out for a drink, so they weren't even in on a Sunday – and the small number that did turn up never liked the big room upstairs. Its size and airiness is why it was perfect for anti-covid measure but made it impossible to create the cosiness they treasured.

There were no allies around the room. What to do.

We could just refuse to move back into the bar. The club had no money before but with so long a period of closure it was now just weeks away from running out of money without our cash flow support, and the members who might come in and volunteer to run it if we refused were mostly shielding. It wouldn't take a lot to force it through. But it would be like using a sledgehammer on a picture hook and the principle of being in service to everyone would be smashed. Everyone gets what they want.

Joanna was trying to get President Terry to stop calling her a girl. Enough.

'Okay Terry. We'll move it downstairs. I want to make it clear that there isn't room for everyone who came last Sunday in the chairs that we can have downstairs. You will have to turn people away. You understand that right?'

'It's just not right having the girls carrying drinks upstairs. It's unladylike.'

Deafness had come over him again.

We moved it all around in time for the next Sunday. The two downstair public rooms are windowless, and with tables at 2m apart we could fit maybe forty people in total.

The bar staff couldn't get the members to obey any of the rules. It's a lot to ask someone on £9.20 an hour to physically throw out seventy-five-year-old men who refuse to sit at the table they've been assigned. We were terrified of an outbreak of Covid in this membership – we might not always agree with them, but we desperately didn't want any of them dead.

So, Joanna and I took it in turns to police Sundays. Spending twelve hours on a Sunday explaining over and over again to men with 'I want my country back' pins on their flat caps that they needed to stay in their seats, stop sitting more than six to a table and let us take their temperatures on the way in. The same arguments with the same people each week.

'This is my club!'

'This is all of our club. And you are most welcome. You just have to give your name and address at the door – it's test and trace rules.'

'You enjoy this. It makes you feel powerful.'

'Yes, I love spending twelve hours arguing with pensioners that they should obey public health rules. If I'd known this was a career option twenty years ago, I'd need never have spent the time becoming a theatre director.'

Over and over again. For a couple of weeks, the received wisdom was that Covid was an attempt to stop Brexit.

I laughed.

'What's so funny?'

'Well amongst much else, the idea that this Government is competent enough to do all this and keep it a secret. It's just such a testament to your faith in government.'

'I think Boris is doing a good job.'

'Of course you do. I thought he invented this to stop Brexit?'

'Not him! The Europeans did it.'

'Okay, but you're still not coming in until I've taken your temperature, Jim.'

It was a sickening situation. With limited space available to sit people, we hadn't even bothered telling the wider public we were open again – there was nowhere to put anyone new. We were expanding a massive amount of energy and money running a bar – badly.

The only logical thing to do was close it down – like many of the other pubs in the city. Write it off as a bad job until we could reopen properly.

But that would have broken the promise we'd made. We'd promised we'd look after the club for them. And I was damned if we were going to break the promise.

There are moments when keeping our promises feels Quixotic. But keeping your promises when it's easy is hardly a challenge.

AN ART GALLERY ON THE LAMP POSTS

A few years ago, we were doing a show called *Flood*, for Hull UK City of Culture 2017. It required us to learn a whole host of new things; how to drive safety boats, operate telehandlers, abseil, fire shotguns, all sorts of new skills.

And when we returned from these courses, we sometimes found ourselves strangely unprepared. We'd learnt new things, but normally just enough to ensure that the liability would be ours if something went wrong. Nearly every course had at least four hours' study on the 1974 Health and Safety at Work Act which was designed to cover everyone's arses apart from whoever it was wielding the chainsaw, or telehandler. Education as a way to pass on liability, not knowledge.

We got talking about adult education, about the marketisation of universities and what that had done to the student-lecturer relationship.

When I was a kid, my mum did woodworking courses with the Women's Institute; but now the WI was a part of the social care emergency services, all foodbanks and fundraising drives.

There was cultural adult education still, but it was often expensive, well beyond the reach of a large part of society. Certainly, beyond the financial reach of any of us working at Slung Low.

And so much else seemed to be focused on 'side hustles', yet more ways of making money from your leisure time. Where did people who weren't wealthy go to learn things for the joy of learning them, of expanding themselves, of finding one less thing in the world to be scared of?

In response to all this thinking, we opened a Pay What You Decide Cultural Community College a few years before the Coronavirus crisis. It taught everything from bread baking, to how to use a compass, from south Indian cooking to Irish dancing. And much else in between.

We started with star gazing. Knowledge that a few thousand years ago would have had you burned as a witch or heretic or lauded as a god, was now pointless in a monetary, side hustle sense but still transformative to your mind. Stand in the middle of a field and know your place in the universe.

The college has proved popular. Fire eating, black smithying, film making, classes full of people trying something new.

Thanks to the vagaries of the government rules, the college was the first thing back in operation in that first lockdown. Spoon whittling live streamed from the Slung Low wood, Facebook Indian cooking with Manjit's Kitchen, people back connecting with each other. It was in large part because the foodbank had kept us open throughout that we were able to quickly put on events online or in-person when the opportunity presented itself. If we'd been starting from a standing start of having mothballed operations, I'm not sure we would have been able to do as much as we did that summer.

One thing that definitely came out of the opportunities and provocations afforded by our new social care role was the LS11 Art Gallery. As we delivered food, we'd noted how scared people were. Even on the phone. I'd done a couple of deliveries to some club members who were normally full of attitude and beans and been shocked at how cowed they were. The national health messaging was vital, but it had resulted in people being scared into their homes. Retreating from the world in all sorts of mental and emotional ways as well as physical ones.

LS11 Art Gallery was a response to that. The team had come up with it, I hadn't been taken with it at first. Sounded chip shop. Not the sort of thing we did, which goes to show how much I know.

The idea was simple. We would put a letter through every door in the area saying we understood that people had to stay at home and isolate and folk were worried, but they were still brilliant, still creative, still capable. And if they made a piece of art, a painting or drawing or photograph then they could call us on our foodbank number and we would come and take a photo of it.

Then we'd print that image on a big weather-proof board and display it on the lampposts around the area.

It proved incredibly popular. People were over the moon to have some way of connecting with others. The City Council Culture Department liked the idea and stumped up the money to print the boards.

But it was the quality of the work that was really surprising. In all sorts of styles and forms it was fascinating and brilliant.

Up the printed boards went on the lampposts and people on their Boris bimble and got to see the brilliance of their neighbours.

It was joyful. Many of the pieces now take pride of place on the walls of the theatre upstairs at the club.

The press got interested and the local BBC News telly programme did a piece. I missed the piece when it aired because I was having a bath. And whilst I was having that bath, my phone rang.

'Is this Alan Lane?'

'Yes.' These calls are never good news. I've never won something in a prize draw I've forgotten entering.

'I'm the principal lamp post engineer for the city of Leeds.'

'Okay.' Is that a thing? I had no idea.

'I've just watched a piece on Look North about your lamp post art gallery.'

'Great.' Maybe it is good news after all.

'No, not great.' Okay maybe not then. 'You're going to have to take it all down.'

And there began a very long conversation about how waterproof boards attached to lamp posts offer the potential for serious damage to both property and persons and how the disregard we had shown to the safety of the people of Leeds in our unilateral cultural activity was bordering on the criminal, and so on and so forth.

I was tired, in the bath and at this point of the crisis, bored of being shouted at by members of the public. Members of the public who thought I WAS the city council and bored of being talked to like an idiot by members of the city council because they thought I worked for THEM.

It was this tiredness that caused me to let him finish his long bollocking, before explaining that I would happily take them all down immediately (after my bath naturally) but the work was actually financially supported by the City Council and in that sense had been commissioned by the council itself. And given that the very leader of the council, Judith Blake, held the cultural portfolio that really it was her who commissioned this, in one sense at least, and so it was her we should be ringing at *checks watch* 7:30 on a Thursday evening to get approval to dismantle it and did he, Chief-Lamp-Post-Engineer such as he was, want to ring Councillor Blake or should I?

And then we started our conversation again from the point of view of being two people who had the other in a choke grip and only gently, and with abundant mutual good faith, would we get out of it both of us intact.

He was a lovely man.

And not unreasonably concerned that some lunatic was going around wrecking lamp posts. Crucially we had good paperwork explaining how we'd put the signs up (well above head height, perpendicular to the road, using an A-frame ladder that didn't lean against the lamp post, in case anyone is thinking of giving it a go) and after a little while we put all our weapons down and agreed that we were all winners here and that I wouldn't do it again without letting him know.

One of my favourite things about the LS11 Art Gallery is that quite often the boards would go missing. But you wouldn't find them on the road nearby, discarded. They'd be taken somewhere by someone who wanted the art. People were stealing the art of their neighbours because they wanted to look at it more often.

And the second thing I would love is that when these thefts happened the people who lived near where the stolen art used to be would call us. Complaining that someone had stolen the art that was outside their house. And telling us that they wanted it back.

And we would replace it with a new print. Because that's what you do in a gallery.

People are brilliant. Even when they are stuck in their house scared. It's particularly important in those moments that they realise how brilliant they are. And, for a bit, reminding them was our job.

SNOOKERED

The reopening of the bar had created a number of tensions. Getting the members to obey government guidelines became a repetitive strain on the team, as we spent our Sundays doing our best to keep them safe and vaguely in check. And the refusal to accept the bar upstairs had left us with a lack of space.

We had solved the problem by moving the whole foodbank into the snooker room. The snooker room was the pride and joy of a small number of the members. A dozen men who had been members for decades who would spend an hour on a Saturday evening, and occasionally on a Sunday, playing snooker with each other on two full sized tables. It was quite the bragging rights locally that the club still had two full sized tables.

We covered the tables with boards to protect the green and then piled boxes of cereals and bagels on top. Crates of tins sat around the outsides of the room and a mountain of toilet rolls in the corner. Scrunching the whole foodbank into the one room was hard, but it was the only place left after the decision about upstairs.

It also meant that for the foreseeable that the snooker room was out of action. I had assumed that as snooker was still forbidden by the government and (even in pre-Covid times) it was only used an hour or two a week, this wouldn't be a major problem. Once again, I had misunderstood the situation and underestimated how much trouble a dozen or so men could cause us.

There was an immediate outcry on Facebook and then in the club. The men who enjoyed the snooker room were furious, which I was expecting, but so were other members.

'You don't even play snooker!'

'It's the principle of the thing.'

'What's the principle?'

'We should be able to use the snooker room if we want to.'

'In an ideal world yes, but it's pretty unusual times.'

'Why should us members, who own the club, give up what is ours for other people? You're not delivering food to me, are you?'

'Well I would if you want it.'

'I don't.'

'Okay but, and I don't think this is remotely the point, I deliver food to over a dozen members and,' I continue looking around the room, 'I deliver to three people sitting in the bar right now.' It was Sunday evening and as full as we could be under new rules.

'I don't believe you. Everyone knows you only deliver food to the blacks.'

And there it was. Even after two years in the place, the sheer stupidity capable within these zero-sum culture war arguments never failed to stop me dead.

I dug my heels in. There was plenty of 'it's damaging the reputation of the club having a food bank here' chat, which failed to understand the nature of our reputation pre-Covid and, even when I showed them articles in numerous national newspapers praising us, the 'damage to reputation' argument continued.

It was £8 an hour at the nearest snooker club and annual membership of The Holbeck was only £6. I wondered whether explaining how great the situation was normally and begging their patience during the crisis would work. I tried it. It didn't. It was apparently the principle of the thing.

The date when the government was going to allow snooker again was fast approaching and I was still nowhere with it. The Facebook complaints became overwhelming. I stopped answering the comments for the first time, as it just took up too many hours. One of the more aggressive members started demanding to see the contracts between the club and Slung Low. There was no worry from a legal point of view, but folks asking for contracts only leads to more work.

It had become a totemic issue in which no one was willing to be reasonable. The club was only being financially kept afloat by Slung Low. Slung Low was only able to do that because of a new-found purpose of social care providers. With Covid looking to stretch long into the future, the foodbank was the frog and the snooker players were the scorpion. If they were ever going to get back to playing in that room, they needed the foodbank. Apparently they weren't scared of the water, because they kept the pressure up on us.

It reached a head one Sunday evening. One of the senior members shouted into Joanna's face, 'I'd rather burn the place down to the ground then let you keep us out of the snooker room.'

It's no surprise that they keep their most outrageous and physically aggressive behaviour for when the six foot three Army Reserve Officer isn't in the building and when only the women of Slung Low are present. But we are talking about an organisation who've only allowed women members for last forty years. So none of this is accidental.

Anyway, this was a step too far and an escalation. Something had to be done, it couldn't carry on like this.

Next morning the team discussed leaving the club. We had the money to leave. Our commitment was to Holbeck, Slung Low could survive without The Holbeck. The club would be bankrupt within a month without us. We could probably buy it in a few weeks.

That would be a failure. Our failure. Our mission of Cultural Democracy dead.

But we couldn't carry on having people being shouted at. Did we have the energy to keep going? Yes, but we had to squash the snooker room issue. It was the wrong hill to die on. If culture is decided by everyone then it was only fair that this small group of selfish, aggressive men get to decide what their culture was as well. And they had decided it was this snooker room. Everyone gets what they want.

We needed a logistical solution. Ruth Saxton got on the phone to our pals at Leeds United. They were sponsored by Clipper – global logistics experts. They could provide a refrigerated container for the car park. And they could do it for free, because they understood how important the food was to those we were delivering.

We were going to have to put in external specialist power. A big new commando socket on the outside wall. And that was going to cost a few thousand pounds. Sucking it up, we found the money from reserves – Joanna magicking it up from wherever she does that stuff. It was a solution. It left a bitter taste in the mouth, but it would do everything everyone wanted.

And then the day came that everything in the snooker room had to be moved into the lorry. We were absolutely knackered, the volunteers had already headed home and the physical metaphor of having to drag every tin, every box out of the club and into the lorry was just too much. I was beat and furious, at them, at myself, at the whole situation. Furious that a place that had stood for 140 years as a palace of mutual helpfulness was expelling a foodbank that delivered hundreds of parcels a week so a handful of people could play snooker. I didn't have the energy.

And then some old friends arrived. Paul and Mandy with their family, three generations of members who had welcomed our arrival, who had come to shows and events, who we'd become friends with. They'd come down to do a shift in the foodbank. They were the cavalry. They started lifting and shifting. Stayed the whole afternoon. Got it all done. Tonnes of food lifted into the lorry.

They were the daughter and sons, granddaughters and grandsons of one of the snooker players.

I have no idea whether they came because they knew, or whether they could see we were beat and needed reinforcements, or just because they thought it was their turn to come in. I didn't ask them. I was just thankful.

It all fitted into the lorry and the new model of working began.

We hoovered the snooker room, returned cues to their places and waited for the players to arrive.

In the months that the government allowed snooker that year, there was a total of four hours of snooker played in those rooms.

It turned out it really was the principle for those men. Their room was open again. They didn't feel the need to go into it.

Everybody gets what they want. That's a rule. Thanks to our pals at Leeds United and Clipper nobody got to stop anyone else getting what they wanted. It didn't feel like a victory, but it was. We had kept the show on the road.

INGRAM ROAD PRIMARY SCHOOL

I think every Artistic Director of a publicly funded theatre should be a governor at their local primary school. Many of them are.

I am very honoured to be a governor at Ingram Road Primary School.

It's on the other side of the Moor and run by a brilliant headteacher called Sarah Millard. She is a take-no-nonsense, thoughtful, determined woman who leads a school with a whole host of challenges. Forty languages are spoken in the school. One class concluded Year 6 without any of the original class members who started in reception, such is the change and churn of Holbeck.

OFSTED has not always been overly enamoured with the school, but I am and that's because me and OFSTED don't share an understanding of what this school needs and the community it sits in.

It was for these kids that we turned one of our old touring shows into an illustrated hardback book. I was sat in Sarah's office one day, discussing food deliveries and she mentioned that there were children in school who had not one book at home, and if it wasn't for the school's policy of awarding books as prizes whenever they can, these kids would head to secondary school still book-less.

I headed back to the club and told the team the story.

'Well, we can do something about that easily enough,' said Producer Joanna before commissioning designer Heledd Rees to draw the pictures to John Hunter's new adaptation of a show we used to tour to theatres, *Emergency Story Penguin*.

Emergency Story Penguin reveals that all theatres have secret submarines in their basements so they can respond to a story emergency at a moment's notice anywhere in the world. As the children are being shown around the submarine a report of a penguin stranded on a piece of melting ice comes in and there's no alternative but to set off in the sub and rescue it. The tale is of the risk of global warming but it's really a book about the importance and power of stories.

It was perfect for the moment and for these kids particularly. The book came back from the printers gleaming and we gave every kid in the school a free copy. Then launched an online fundraiser to ensure that every single primary school child in Holbeck would get a free copy of the book before Christmas. They did.

I was in to see a class once and the teacher asked the kids if they knew who Slung Low were.

Yes, replied the first hand in the air, you put on that play with singing that I saw at the club.

Yes, replied the second hand in the air, you made that book that I got to take home.

Yes, replied the third hand in the air, you deliver my food on a Wednesday.

Sarah Millard and the school are our most important food partner in Holbeck.

Surprisingly, the hardest thing about being a food hub is not finding the food. There's lots about and you can always buy it wholesale if you are desperate. No, the hardest thing is finding homes for the food when a glut comes in. We'd often be winding down for the day when Leeds Rhinos would arrive with a van of something, or Leeds United with several hundred litres of soured cream, or The Real Junk Food Project with 200 loaves of bread. In order to continue to be a reliable partner to all those who found themselves surprised by 1000 avocados a few hours ago, you have to have someone to give it to. It's too great a failure to throw away food in a world of hungry people. That's not acceptable.

And in the school we had a large number of willing participants. For months we would deliver the glut of cheesecakes and dinner rolls from Costco to the school along with vegetables for their healthy eating stall and get cheered like heroes for it.

And it flowed the other way. I lost track of the number times I would get a message from Sarah, explaining that the staff room was full (again) of boxes of bagels and porridge. Was it possible to send the van round so teachers could get to their pigeon-holes? It saved our bacon so many times.

Over the course of this crisis, we had got good at finding large amounts of food and getting that food to people who might need it as quickly as possible. But in Sarah and her staff we found people with expert, granular knowledge about the needs of so many of our immediate community. When we were accused of giving too much food to those who didn't necessarily need it, we could always point to, and be reassured by, the forensic targeting of Sarah and her understanding of the need in her families.

Time and time again the steel of Sarah's leadership was inspiring. A lighthouse that helped in finding our way through these new responsibilities.

This kind of thoughtful care and pragmatism is what Holbeck needs and without her the area would be so much poorer. In a town that seems to be endlessly rowing, she rises above the tawdry arguments, putting the welfare of her children first every time.

We don't have many people in Holbeck who have the ability to see another's point of view. Sarah is a rare and precious leader.

MANNA FROM MECCA

'Mecca want to give us a load of hot meals every day.'

'Mecca?'

'The bingo people.'

'Hot meals?'

'They're not open anymore and they have freezers full of meals and they've been given permission to cook them and give them to us.'

So, every day for months at midday, a team of volunteers would head off to the bingo hall and fill their takeaway delivery thermo bags with meals in polystyrene trays. The meals were what you would expect from a bingo hall. Sausage and chips, pie and chips, burger and chips. Chips.

And then as fast as they could, the volunteers would dash their cars to their lists of addresses of families. From our various partners we'd created a list of sixty-five children who we would deliver these hot meals to every day. What they lacked in vegetables and nutritional balance they made up for in taste and excitement. If you've never delivered high-fat, high-salt content lunches to incredibly bored and very often incredibly hungry children in the middle of a pandemic, then you've not fully experienced the joy of people genuinely thrilled to see you.

Children would rush from the door and grab the food trays from the delivery drivers' hands. It hardly fitted with our push to healthy eating but the glee the food brought was hard not to fill you heart with joy.

In the end the bingo halls would prepare to open again and the something meaty with chips would end but for many weeks it was an incredibly useful supplement to the food parcels.

They also put us in touch with families on a daily basis. This proved to be vital. Once the food parcels were running smoothly, we had started to do more for their general health and mental well-being, like sending out creativity packs to families, or assisting with digital poverty.

But after a few weeks of delivering the hot meals, to the same families, at the same time every day, we noticed a change. Despite the initial joy, it became clear that things were on the decline. As each day went by the kids were slightly more hectic, the parents a touch more tense. As the summer wore on, the tension increased. There was talk of street fights and a worry about some sort of outbreak, a summer riot.

We got talking to some of the parents. There was nothing for the kids to do. They were tired of trying to keep their children in tiny houses with nothing to do. Things were starting to get worn and tight.

Wrongsemble are a brilliant theatre company that specialise in theatre for children and have their office upstairs at the club. We concocted a plan to perform a play for the kids we delivered food to. We'd use a lorry as a stage in the car park outside the club. In usual times our shows are performed using a headphone system – the actors wear microphones and the audience sit at a distance listening through headphones, like a pirate radio station. This meant we could keep plenty of distance between the audience and the performers, which removed one problem. Then if we were going to manage to do this safely, we were going to have to keep the audience from each other. We had fencing that we could use to create 3m grids for families to sit in. Each grid would sit a little blue tent. With everyone facing the same way they would be protected from each other. With many more event staff than we'd ever usually employ plus all the other mitigations, we were confident we could keep everyone happy.

We would only invite families individually – no marketing campaign – we'd know exactly who was coming and how we'd welcome them and keep them safe.

So, we prepared the event paperwork, let the local authorities know what we are up to and set about going through our preparations.

I was reasonably sure what we were doing would be fine by the legislation, but it took a little careful tiptoeing around the gaps in guidance. Nothing was mentioned directly so we cracked on and waited for someone to say something. We prepared our arguments just in case. Everyone seemed happy and the great day arrived. We spent the morning turning the car park into a socially distanced auditorium.

And then, four hours before we were due to perform, the Culture Secretary announced that he was hopeful that socially distanced outdoor performances would be allowed in a few weeks' time.

Hang on, what now? I couldn't see anywhere in the regulations where it said that socially distanced outdoor performance for small invited audiences weren't allowed, but it was clear that the Culture Secretary thought otherwise. The implication of something being allowed in a few weeks is that it is currently not allowed now. Which was a problem for our fast-approaching performance.

We were in deep now. Nothing to do but push on. The families arrived, the show opened, great delight was had by all. They left. We cleaned the place down. And waited for incoming.

In the end nearly everyone was happy enough with us. The care and detail we had demonstrated was clear to everyone. We weren't trying to make money (the whole event had been free) or open a regular offer to growing audiences – we were just doing what we'd been doing for the last few months, looking after our neighbours the best way we knew how.

Word reached me a week later than by coincidence some of the city's arts leaders had met that evening after our show. The great and good had been furious about the impact it might have to the reputation to the arts generally.

It was the first of many outdoor shows that year, as the rules changed and allowed drive-through shows followed by socially distanced outdoor shows.

The group of kids from that first rare show would come back time and time again to see all sorts, operas and comedies, gameshows and plays.

The *Financial Times* published a drone picture of the whole set-up, lines of blue tents in front of a lorry stage and it wasn't long before companies and theatres from all over the country were getting in touch asking for our event plan and working method statements.

It would seem that the reputation of the city's art sectors had managed to survive us.

CORPORATE GREED SOCIAL FEEDING

In January 2021 the country woke up to the reality of corporations' place in social food. People were outraged at pictures of free school meals being sent to families after the school's closed for lockdown three. Tuna stuffed into coin bags, tomatoes cut in half, the snideness of the food compounded by the idea that this was meant to be £30 worth of food. The companies responsible flapped about making excuses, promising investigations as to how something like this could possibly have happened. And yet many of us were not in the least bit surprised. This wasn't a failing of the system, this was parts of the system revealed suddenly by the shift to home-schooling. Because what had caused this was not individuals' decisions or a failure of supply. It was the inevitable consequence of introducing profit into a process designed to provide food for those who can't provide it for themselves.

Our van proved to be the most useful part of our shifting to social food provision. So many food banks and similar projects are run by individuals, out of homes or garages, using their own cars to do what they can in their spare time. And then we came along with a transit van and full-time staff who could guarantee to be where they meant to be week in week out. Our friend in the Salvation Army, the mighty Mark Hodgkinson wondered if we wanted to take the Wednesday and Friday slots at the cash & carry Costco.

(Mark, among other wonderful acts, later organised a brass band to drive around the ward on the top deck of a double decker bus spreading Christmas cheer, but for now his mind was on excess food.)

Every morning Costco would have a pile of excess food that needed to be removed from the premises, and each day a different charity would have the slot to come and fetch it. With the lockdown many of the charities, run by elderly or vulnerable volunteers, were not available to fetch the food.

Sounded like a dream opportunity to us. The only rule, Mark explained, was that you had to take everything they left out for you. All of it. Not a problem, we've a van. They can be a bit funny, Mark warned, but there's plenty of food on offer.

He was right. There were often lots of exciting things – cakes, meat, all sorts of good stuff. One Wednesday there were two dozen Gressingham ducks, which led to us driving around Beeston, time running out on us, trying to get rid of these ducks.

'What do you do with a duck?' asked one woman.

'Cook it like a chicken, eat it like a king!' we shouted as we left one on her doorstep and sped off to the next address.

But amongst the ducks and cheeseboards there was also piles of nonsense. Mouldy stuff. Packs of butter with boot prints in them where they had been kicked along the warehouse floor.

And the rule was indeed that you had to take it all. So, we often had to pay to have it removed from the club by waste disposal. A cost that should have been Costco's – £300 a tonne. Except their charitable giving saved them the cost and passed it to us.

Every week the same stuff. How do we have algorithms that can tell you the exam results of unborn children, but Costco didn't understand that every Wednesday they would fail to sell nineteen huge cheesecakes, 600 dinner rolls and fifty bags of mouldy lettuce? What always frustrated me was that all this stuff was dated the day we fetched it and we'd race around desperately trying to get rid of it, or have to pay to have it removed. And yet I knew (after a few months it was obvious) that Costco knew the day before, the day before the day before, that this stuff wasn't needed.

They didn't care enough to bother. The imagination just wasn't there. They had found a way to pass their removal costs to food banks and look good doing it.

Yet with this waste food I could feed many families. It was discarded, sitting in the sun in the car park in trolleys waiting for us. This, this little thing, makes a difference to a family between having enough and smiling at each other or being hungry, tired, angry.

We would always send Matt to fetch the Costco food. I've never met anyone who didn't find Matt agreeable and the people in charge of the charitable giving at Costco were strange, combative: Matt was the right antidote to such a situation. I hoped in time he might soften them. He didn't, but Matt is built to ignore combativeness. So, we all buggered on together until the summer.

And then one day in July, Matt's daughter was sick and of course he wasn't available. I didn't want to miss the food, so I jumped in the van and set off to Costco. As I arrive one of the forklift lads recognises the van and shouted, 'this is yours here!' pointing at a few trolleys piled high with food. I started loading it all into the van. There was some good stuff here – those cheesecakes again – but also huge tubs of coleslaw and potato salad which had smashed open on the car park floor. Nothing I can do with that, I thought.

'WHO ARE YOU?'

I turn to face the shouting woman. She was the Costco staff member in charge of the charities fetching the waste food.

'Hello.'

'Who are you? Who are you?' She seemed to be very keen to know who I was. We had met many times previously but clearly, she had forgotten. She was loud, aggressive and rude.

With a flourish I slide the van door shut revealing the massive logo on the side. Slung Low. I point at the logo with all the elan of Michael Ball closing his one man show with a cover of 'Don't Rain on My Parade'.

We were barred from the Costco in the time it took me to drive back to the club.

I had fucked it up. It was classic arrogance on my part. Costco had no problem being rude to us because they had no respect for us, for any of the people who were desperately trying to feed the families, who couldn't afford to buy food from a place like Costco. Just as whoever it was who stuffed that tuna into the coin bag didn't have any respect for whoever was going to have make their kid's lunch with it. But the person in my role needs to lower their eyes and put up with it if they want the food.

But I hadn't. And now there would be a whole load of families that wouldn't be getting huge cheesecakes and brie wheels the size of your head. And that was on me for sure.

But it's also on Costco.

TELLING STORIES

At the last election we were asked to host the filming of a Labour Party broadcast. We said yes. On the day a really lovely family from the North East, a nurse from Scotland and a very friendly film crew from London turned up.

They turned the nice lights off, moved furniture and set things up to make the place look bleak.

The ad was about how difficult things were under the Tories. And so the place had to look like it was unloved and crap. I understood. It was a shame, because we had just finished cleaning up after a bumper weekend of shows, workshops and people's celebrations and if I'd known they were going to grotty the place up I could have left the sausage rolls and Bombay mix on the carpet.

I got chatting to one of those in charge on a tea break.

'I heard this place had an amazing cabaret here last week.'

'Oh yeah, it was heaving. Everyone was here.'

'Nice, breathing life back into the place.'

'Yeah, but it's not just shows. We run classes, host mutual aid groups, football fans, bingo, all sorts.'

'Great.'

'And all because of a set of values, lefty principles coupled with state subsidy: Labour principles.'

'Yeah! Great!'

'The ad could be about projects like this – that only happen in spite of this government and its policies but should be, and would be with a Labour government, happening in all communities.'

'Ah,' he said laughing, 'you don't know much about politics.'

And off he pootled.

Maybe I don't know much about politics, but I do know about storytelling. And the consistently depressing one that has been told by the left for the last ten years or more is a terrible story.

Everyone is the hero of their own narrative, no one thinks they are an extra in the epic of world news.

Too often there is no room in the narrative of the Labour Party for people like us here in Holbeck to feel heroic, like they mattered, like they could take action and have an impact.

This was so clear during the Brexit campaign. One of the safest Labour seats in the country and yet the club was mostly full of vocal Brexiters. They hadn't just voted Brexit, they could not wait for it to come, eager for their freedoms.

'Do you think that it will affect your second home in Tenerife?' I would ask President Terry from time to time. A number of the elderly gentlemen members who came in on a Sunday morning for a pint and a game of cards would spend a large number of months abroad on the Spanish islands in their second homes. The pins on their flat caps might decry 'we want our country back' but it would appear on a ¾ timeshare basis only: the rest of the time they were very happy living in someone else's.

There was absolutely no discrepancy in this logic for the members that were vocally enthusiastic about Brexit. You might start the conversation with immigration, or fishing quotas, or even bananas but it would always end in the same place – they were having an impact. They were sticking it to the man. Exactly who the man was and what he had done to them was never clear. How the man didn't include the old Etonian, Oxford graduate Alexander Boris de Pfeffel Johnson was also unclear.

But none of that mattered. I could argue with them all I wanted, and I mostly didn't want to, because it made no difference. They had won. Change would come. Because of them. That was their victory and any discussion was just sore losing on my part. They were the heroes in their story: active, certain, defiant. At last.

Over the years, other things would get wrapped up in this narrative; too many queer acts in a cabaret, the time we served curry three events on the bounce, Covid social distancing rules, Boff Whalley's choir singing about using Boris Johnson's head as a mop. They were all loosely collected in the same category of 'unwanted things being done to us.' There's no arguing with logic like that and it was hard not to be offended by the clear distrust (and often dislike) that was apparent in many of the more established members, especially after everything we'd gone through to bring financial security to the club. There was a naivety to their logic: many of these things they railed against were necessary, laws of the land that had to be obeyed like Covid regulations, and some of them were the cost of no longer being able to be independent of everyone else and hold the space alone. The club's survival was contingent upon collaborating, and that meant compromising. The scorpion raging that it was only political correctness gone mad that he couldn't sting the frog.

But I also felt for them. Men, mostly men, loudly men, who had got to the last chapter of their lives and felt like society didn't really have any need for them anymore. And they found themselves criticised in a language they didn't understand, and for thinking and behaviours that they had always used.

In their minds, and in direct antagonism to the evidence of the communities around them, they were the hardest done by group in the land – even their Brexit victory ruined by Covid and its lockdown.

Of course, this wasn't true. In an area of genuine biting poverty these superannuated men with enough money to buy pints of beer for hours at a time were far from the bottom of the pile. But it didn't need to be true, because it was felt sincerely. It was *their* truth.

For this small group the transformation of the club's fortunes wasn't a collaboration of resources and needs in a brilliant piece of strategy by themselves and their committee but a forced humiliation, a partnership with the woke, the queer, the black.

Because the story being told to these men was that this was what was happening all over the country to good men like them. They were having their rights robbed. That's where those free twenty-five pints had gone. Stolen. By those who didn't understand how these things worked. Or specifically in Holbeck by us, by Slung Low.

The story is so loudly told, so powerfully presented and so seductive to them that they had forgotten that this had been their decision. Unanimous. They couldn't even allow themselves to take credit for saving their own club from closure – they had been forced to do it.

And so, every battle for them was a bridge too far. A hill they were willing to die on. Where the bike shed was going to be placed. The new ale that replaced the no-longer-available Stones. Christmas opening hours. Nothing was just the best decision possible in an imperfect world, but a new slight that could not possibly be accepted.

The team left the city a few months after we moved in to visit a theatre festival. We were only gone a few days but in that time President Terry with some other committee members had gone down the council offices to get the licence changed so they could open early, in order to attract the breakfast crowd on their way to an early kick off at Elland Road. That's not how licences work and they were sent on their way. But not before the Licensing Department had called us to express concern at these two agitated men's demand. An embarrassment to be chided by the authorities so.

We'd have to talk to the discontented.

'Why didn't you just talk to us about it?'

'It's not the point, we should be able to change the licence whenever we want.'

'It isn't your licence!'

'It's our club!'

'It's all of our club.'

On a point of fact, we were both right. When we moved into the club the licence had been changed to a public licence, held by Joanna, rather than a members only club licence.

The new licence, amongst other benefits around theatre performances, meant it was much harder to refuse entry to members of the community. To do so now, for any reason, was impossible to hide behind a 'it's members only' rationale. This club that sat in one of the most diverse communities in the city could no longer be available only to those that the committee chose as worthy. Everyone was going to have to be made to feel welcome.

This was the heart of so much of this pain and argument – not the detail of the issues in the moment – but this lack of control. The deal the club had struck was a good one. We invested tens of thousands of pounds almost instantly. The Holbeck was made financially secure for a decade. It had daily professional energy managing it which had already led to so many benefits and improvements. And in return the club's committee and historic members had only to give up one thing. Control of exactly who got to use the space. That was it. They had got everything they wanted but lost the ability to stop other people getting what they wanted, too. And in the end so many of these conversations about Brexit, and more broadly the culture war nonsense, came down to that perceived loss of control.

The stories told to Holbeck, and other places like it, by the left, too often have no room for people to feel heroic in them. And until they do, the stories told by those who offer a central role in return for division will continue to win the day.

TELL ME THIS BEFORE YOU EAT

In the future, one of the hardest things to explain to people will be how during the Covid crisis a decent centre forward for Manchester United and England was one of the country's most important moral leaders.

When so many cultural and political and religious leaders were caught in the headlamps of the crisis and prayed, they were frozen between the wheels as Covid rushed over them, Marcus Rashford demonstrated clarity, compassion and the ability to tell a good story to provoke change. He was the hero of the moment and what the moment needed. His ability to draw attention to food poverty and the systems that keep people in food poverty was brilliant and his commitment to making a change was galvanising.

Naturally, like any intervention from without a system, Rashford's campaign relied on the mainstream stalwarts of the foodbank system; Trussell Trust and Fare Share.

This is the only sensible option for a broad consensus campaign like his.

But for those of us who were already in the system, these were often problematic partners. Fairshare couldn't, in accordance with their own rules, provide food to Slung Low. In large part these are political questions – neither organisation believe in non-means tested self-referral foodbanks. These organisations exist within the current political system, so systems that look to disrupt the structures that keep people in 'just in time' food poverty are not able to access their services.

If there are two organisations that will give you food, but one requires you to fill in forms and demonstrate your poverty, while the other will just give you food, people will go to the second one. You can't eat dignity, but food tastes better if you're allowed to keep it. So many organisations like Slung Low had seen an explosion in referrals. They removed the barriers to food but were locked out of the system that Rashford has flushed with food and money, because they refused to obey rules that got in the way of hungry people getting food. Such is the nature of the world. It's okay. But it made the job harder.

And then the Council decided to broker a relationship between us, and the other Community Volunteer Hubs, and Fare Share, which was huge news. The ability to access this supply of food would make a huge difference to us, making things much easier.

All we had to do was sign a supply agreement.

In the agreement was the commitment that we would ask each referral five questions.

1. What is the reason for your crisis?

2. How long do you feel you might need some help for?

3. What support would help to alleviate your crisis?

4. Have you contacted any other services for help?

5. Have you been to any other food provider?

We couldn't do this.

The premise of the questions assumes this was a passing temporary crisis. And one that could be solved by the proper usage of the current support system. That the Department of Works and Pensions was our saviour. This is, take it from a man who has spent hours trying to navigate the benefits system on behalf of others, arrant nonsense.

The people who receive our food aren't lazy. They aren't stupid. They were born in a society where the inequalities of funding, of education, of health provision, of opportunity are so profound that the hill they have to climb is steeper than is reasonable. They live in a society that has encouraged zero-hour contract working with the lie of freedom and choice and now believes that the reason so many children of these workers, who find themselves with unreliable incomes, irregular hours and an administratively cruel benefits system, are hungry is because of a temporary crisis. The crisis wasn't and isn't temporary. It isn't a crisis. It's a way of living. An enforced way of living.

Having spent so much energy in removing the barriers to food, here were five more barriers. We couldn't undo all the battles we'd had to get to this point.

Practically, how on earth were we ever going to find the time to ask all these questions? And report the answers? 1500 questions and answers a week. This was a system created by people with different working days than ours.

We couldn't do this. Which meant we couldn't have the FareShare food. It was maddening. We would still do all our deliveries, we would still make sure the hundreds of families that relied upon us got their food, but this just made it harder.

Of course, we understood why FareShare wanted them asking. They were making a case to national government about food poverty. I understood their position. I also understood from the years the theatre sector spent trying to convince national government about arts funding, that our well-reasoned well-researched points aren't going to trump their well-entrenched world view. It was vanity to think otherwise.

And these questions only confirmed it – what was the cause of your crisis? Capitalism, you absolute loons. Structural racism, sexism, classism, the north-south divide, an exploitative jobs market, the echoing effect of the British Empire, crony capitalism, the hostile environment and the fact that Jupiter is in retrograde with Saturn – can I help you with anything else?

We wrote to our long-suffering ward councillors, the tirelessly supportive MP Hilary Benn, everyone else we could find at the council. We wrote a blistering blog trying to get a handhold on the debate. We trod a fine line to try and stay on the right side of Rashford's brilliant campaign and also making it clear that perhaps FareShare et al were not the entire answer to the problem of making sure people had enough to eat.

Other community hubs in the city were equally concerned. They wrote a collective letter, they put pressure on. Meanwhile we kept pedalling as fast as we could. Friendly organisations let us know that they just signed the FareShare agreement and then never asked the questions. It was a brilliantly practical solution, but we were already so over-extended with the authorities that signing a contract with the council and FareShare that I had no intention of fulfilling was a risk too far. We had too many people interested in us being brought to heel to give them so easy a way of doing it. Others ordered food with FareShare and then just dropped it off with us: that's the sort of solidarity you can't buy, heroes all. We kept going. We kept our promises.

And then Joanna got a call from one of our council handlers.

'From Monday FareShare will not be requiring partners who receive food from them to ask the five questions.'

'That means we can start getting food from them?'

'Council has already arranged membership of the scheme for every community hub including yours.'

'Why the change in policy?'

'Many reasons, but pressure from Holbeck and Beeston ward was cited as being a large contributing factor.'

'Thanks for letting us know.'

'Keep going.'

They'd changed their mind. The ward councillors had apparently been properly bolshy, we would be told later in excited whispers. They'd obviously been fired up about it by someone.

This job has often felt like tilting at windmills. Once in a while you catch your lance on something and open your eyes to see a giant lying on the floor cursing you.

The trick is to stay on the horse. The FareShare food would help keep us in the saddle.

PETE

A regular arrives at door. We've about ten who come every other day or so. They're homeless, on the verge of homeless or crashing in a squat. This is Pete, well known to us but he's not in a good way today, he's shaky.

'Hi Pete, here's your food.'

'Can I get £20 for electricity too, please?' For a while we'd been giving out £20 cash for electricity and gas. People had donated it to be handed on and we didn't feel comfortable not giving it away. But giving out cash at the door obviously caused entirely predictable issues, so once the funds that had been directly donated for such things had dried up, we stopped doing it. We hadn't done it for weeks, but it didn't stop folk asking. You can't criticise anyone for trying.

'I can't do that Pete. What I can do is send someone to your local shop, get you the electricity on the card and drop the card back off with you.' This was our new approach. It had worked with most people. But not today it seems.

'Just give me the money, Alan.'

'Can't do that pal.'

'You can trust me.'

'Not a matter of trust. I have to get a receipt.'

'I'll get the receipt and bring it back.'

'No need to trouble yourself, I'll send someone.'

'You can trust me.'

'It's not a matter of trust.'

'Come on Alan, just give me the money.'

He's crying now.

'I can't do that.'

'You can trust me.' He's not shouting. Tears rolling down his face. A human desperate. He's working out his options, weight shifting in his body.

'Unclench your fists, Pete. Breathe mate. Just breathe. I'll get your electricity sorted.'

'Just give me the money.' He's up on his toes now. Fist clenched. I will knock him down if he comes for me. If I have to. But I'm hoping it won't be necessary.

'Breathe Pete. Just breathe mate. I can't give you the money. I'll send a driver.'

'You can trust me. Just give me the money.'

'I can't do that. I'll send a driver round to the house to fetch your leccy card. You'll have electricity within half an hour.'

He knows it's a dead end now. He limps away. I send a driver round thirty minutes later. He's not in when driver gets there. I knew he wouldn't be.

That day was the day we bought 300 toys for kids ready for Christmas. We delivered sixty food parcels that day. And I did my day job.

But in bed I was thinking of fake electricity meters and the moment Pete had given up. I'd broken him just by standing there. Refusing to move. It felt like bullying.

Lying in bed that night I wish I'd have just given him the fucking money.

We don't allow 'you can't do this forever' to be the excuse for not doing what is necessary in the moment at Slung Low. We'll work out what to do about the precedent once we've sorted the fire in the bin out.

Freezing in front of a future problem is how we end up with the daily injustice and indignity that Holbeck is full of.

But all that said, it had become clear to us that handing out £20 notes at the fire exit door of a pub to anyone who could say the words 'electricity please' was not sustainable.

We'd run out of money sure, but we'd likely get turned over first. Little did we know then how right we were.

SEX WORKER MANAGED AREA

George was one of the club regulars who came in every Sunday morning. One minute past 11 every Sunday, he would arrive slowly and sit down in the same seat. A large heavy-set man he had been born in Glasgow and still had the accent and general air of the city

Across the room from George would sit another regular, Seamus, an equally affable Irishman. These two would sit and gently throw sectarian insults at each other all morning. 'You fenian!' 'You horrible blue nose you!' I was horrified on that first Sunday morning but soon realised that it was a playful and entirely unaggressive dance that these two did every week. I had bigger problems to deal with and whilst officially it definitely broke our diversity and inclusion policy, this wasn't something I was going to mither myself with and these two men quickly became favourites.

Every week George would order exactly the same drinks at the same time. A can of Irn Bru and a Famous Grouse. It was the only Irn Bru we sold and we stocked it to sell George two of them on a Sunday morning that he would cut with six Famous Grouse before he would stagger home.

One Sunday he didn't turn up. It wasn't a couple of hours before one of the Committee – Nigel an absolute stalwart of the club with his wife Liz – went round to see where he was. George had collapsed, was unconscious and blocking the door from the inside when Nigel arrived. George would make it into hospital but not last for many months. The hearse did a drive-by on the way to the funeral where the team stood in the car park toasting him with an Irn Bru and Famous Grouse.

One of the many things I love about the working men's club idea is that Nigel was there as soon as George wasn't at the club when he was meant to be. There are so many older people in Holbeck who find themselves with no one at the end of their lives. There are organisations in the area to do this work, but they all have a city corporation feel to them: it's charity, not mutual aid.

It might be scant relief to know that if you collapse in your home the men you drink with on a Sunday morning will come and find you, but it is relief nonetheless. And this club, and all the others like it, give that to people who often have no other place to get it. It is in these moments that the purpose and value of the club is so clear.

George was an unbelievably likeable man. He would sit happily for an hour with my little boy, Davidbaby. Davidbaby would sit there chattering away drinking an orange juice and George would sit happily listening and surely not understanding a word, but it didn't seem to bother either of them.

George had problems with incontinence so one of the team would quietly whisk his chair away once he staggered home at 1pm and give it a clean down. Service comes in many forms, some quiet, some loud. This was one of the many quiet ones.

When they found him, he had a box full of cash under his bed. I think that's probably true of a number of our older members, some of whom draw their weekly cash from the till, not trusting the cash machine on the high street.

When he died, we were much more moved than I had thought we would be. In the moment I understood the service we gave to George, the importance of it. But I was also aware that how we'd been running the club, and the amount of time we were spending on a small number of very vocal and often aggressive people meant that we weren't always able to give the time we wanted to other things. Like George. I realised that beyond making sure he was okay, Davidbaby had spent more time talking to him than I ever had. I didn't know much about George and that was clearly a failing.

I did know he had been a steward in the club in past years, living in the flat above the bar that was now artist accommodation. I was also told that his wife had been a victim of the Yorkshire Ripper.

But not much more than that.

The Yorkshire Ripper sits high in the area's cultural landscape here, even after many decades. In large part because violence against women is still a part of our everyday life.

Holbeck has what is called a Managed Area. In this area it is legal (the only part of the UK where this is true) to be a street sex worker or their client. This area was formed because of the historic, over many decades, issues with sex workers and the fact that there were so many acts of violence carried out against them. The Managed Area sits between the residential area of Holbeck and where our old home The HUB was.

On the external wall of The HUB is a beautiful mosaic made by sex workers, in part tribute to one of their number who was murdered a few years back and in part a triumphant celebration of all they are and can be. It is a genuinely moving and handsome piece of art.

When the Managed Area was introduced, we were one of the few organisations who were, broadly speaking, positive about it. We don't need a man talking about the gender politics of sex work and I acquiesce to my female colleagues on that issue. But I am responsible for the safety of a lot of people, many of whom are women, and this scheme made them safer. It is definitely true that other options might make them (and others) even safer but none of those are on offer in Holbeck. I work with what I've got.

The scheme, however, is not universally or even generally popular. It is seen by some as the legalisation of rape and protested by both committed feminists and others who are definitely not. The Managed Area is particularly unpopular with the members of the Club's Committee.

Before we moved in and whilst we were still negotiating the arrangement with the Committee, someone started the rumour that once we were in the club we would use it to serve the sex workers a free breakfast. Something that I have no intention of doing given that we don't provide food, let alone breakfast. It was impossible to scotch this rumour with some members suggesting that I make a statement about the sex workers being unwelcome in the club. Something that would have been immoral, illegal and impossible to actually action.

It is a sign of the current state of discourse around the issue that when we hosted a public meeting on the subject, one of the members of the community felt confident enough to say, in response to being asked what might a solution look like, that – 'What we need is Peter Sutcliffe and his hammer back to sort them out.'

Holbeck can be a cruel place. There is some cruelty in the authorities deciding that here, in this place that has so much to deal with, is where they will try this new experiment. There is immense cruelty to the lives of the women who have to work the streets of Holbeck. And there is monstrous cruelty in how the sex workers are talked about by those who see themselves as leaders in this place. I have never understood why, particularly amongst some of the senior Christians of the area, this issue generates the response it does. Jesus Christ was relatively opaque on many things, but on sex workers he was pretty clear.

I find the issue one of the most complicated of the culture war skirmishes we have here in Holbeck. There is no public meeting, no discussion about anything that will not in short order become about this. It, thanks to a small handful people who are determined and full of angry, righteous zeal on the issue, dominates.

I once asked my friend Sarah Millard, the headteacher of the local primary school, where she stood on the subject. She would not be drawn.

'I have parents here who have come from places, from cultures which means they are very against the whole idea. And I have parents who are sex workers. But mostly I have parents who are just trying their hardest to do right by their kids and for whom this is not the issue they want to spend their time on.'

That is sadly not an option available to any of us here in Holbeck.

MONEY MAKES THE WORLD
GO ROUND

When the council asked us to do this social care job, they immediately paid us £5k. Then they gave us £5k every three months in 2020. In 2021 they gave us £41k for six months.

In total, not including staff costs or premises or vehicles or anything like that, the foodbank operations from March 2020 to June 2021 cost £134,757.45.

The private donations given to us by local and national supporters were £44,871.97.

And the rest is our reserves from being a theatre company and money we could earn from doing talks and teaching classes for universities and drama schools: mostly talking about why a theatre company runs a food bank.

The food boxes changed according to what was available, especially if The Real Junk Food Project had dropped off a lorry load. You might end up with all sorts of exciting things, but every box had as a bare minimum: six pints of milk, loaf of bread, box cereal, six eggs, bag of fresh fruit and veg, bag of dried goods and tins (beans, tomatoes, rice or pasta), sanitary towels. It would usually go out with other things, particularly crisps and chocolate but this was the baseline. We delivered 15,202 of these.

And spent the following on this:

£5,300.03	Eggs (& egg boxes)
£6,868.37	Milk
£3,583.04	Bread

£22,757.41	Tins & Dried Pasta / Rice
£3,753.19	Cereal
£11,729.36	Fresh food
£3,643.28	Misc. food items
£2,835.80	Toilet roll
£3,902.38	Bags
£3,787.77	Misc. items incl. baby products, pet food

MORE PETE

Pete is back. It's been a couple of days since he was in asking for electricity cash. He's calmer now, no longer tight fisted, blood pumping. But he's still anxious.

'Can I have a word, Alan?'

We take a walk around the side of the Foodbank lorry container.

'I need your help.'

'Sure Pete, what is up?'

'I owe a lot of money.'

'Okay.'

'I owe the money to drug dealers.'

'Okay.'

'I owe £200. It's for crack. I don't do smack, I'm not one of them. I don't want you thinking that I am one of them. But I owe a lot of money for crack.'

I hadn't realised there was a moral distinction between a user of crack and a heroin addict but he's adamant that I understand what he's telling me. I do.

I'm waiting for the ask. It always takes a little run up. I'm wondering what we have that can help Pete as he's talking. We don't have £200 and even we can't hand cash to drug dealers but maybe there's something that we can...and then –

'And the dealers have moved into my house. They've thrown me out.'

'Of your house?'

'Yeah. They've got guns. They threw me out. I'm homeless.'

'The drug dealers have thrown you out of your own home?'

'Yes.' He's manic now.

'Okay. Just breathe Pete. We'll work this out. Calm yourself pal.'

'I need your help.'

'Of course, Pete. Of course.'

'Oh, thank God.'

I wasn't expecting this but I'm also relieved. This is something that is easy to help solve. 'This is easy Pete. The inspector of the local police is a friend of ours. This is a matter of a phone call.'

'No! You can't! You can't tell the police. You can't!' He's at a hundred miles an hour now.

'Okay. Okay. It's okay Pete. Just explain what you want.'

'I need your help.'

'To do what?'

'To get rid of them.'

'To get rid of them?'

'Yes.'

I take a moment. I understand how I've come to be stood by the side of refrigerated lorry talking to a crack addict about the gun wielding drug dealers who have taken over his council flat but still, it's a lot in a single moment. It's hard to know what the next thing to say is. I bugger on.

'Pete. You owe two hundred quid for crack. The dealers have moved into your house. And when all that happened you decide your best course of action was to find the local theatre director and ask him to throw the armed criminals out of your home.'

'Yes.'

Mercifully we are both laughing now. I spend the next half an hour urging him to go to the police but he's not having any of it. I'm not 100% certain the story is true – I never am with any of this little group of regular attenders, it rarely is totally true. Pete is emotionally invested in it but that's not quite enough and I've been burned by Pete before. After my best efforts he's gone. He's got an extra-large food package and one of his friends has arrived which means he has somewhere to sleep.

I've no idea what you are meant to do in these moments and it's hectic with everything else, so I push on with deliveries and spend the evening worrying about Pete. It's okay though. He'll be back soon. And he'll find his own solution to his problems.

ERIC AND LEANING IN

In the first week of referrals there was a request to visit a man called Eric who lived in the sheltered accommodation flats not far over the motorway. I went to see Eric and fetch his shopping list. He met me leaning against the door, holding his stick like a rifle. Peeeow! Peeeow! he shouted, and not knowing what else to do I fell to the floor clasping my chest, hit!

He was eighty-three, got angry when I misremembered that as ninety-three, and we would go on to deliver him a food package almost every other day for ten months. Not a full one, just what he needed and special treats that he would firmly request were included – mostly denture fixing and Wispa Bites.

Eric was everybody's favourite. A genuinely pleasant man with tales of a glorious past who had managed to find himself alone and somewhat bereft in a two room flat with no oven. His neighbour was a wrong 'un who took advantage: and Eric was clever enough to know it and lonely enough not to be able to do anything about it.

I lent in. Everyone sent with food was told to find ten minutes to listen to his stories, please.

At the beginning of the crisis, we had – with the team and at home – long conversations about the risks we were taking in staying open. I didn't know how bad it was going to get, none of us did, but I knew we were being prepared to be mobilised in the Army Reserves and the old hands told stories of moving cattle corpses in the foot and mouth crisis. Italy showed pictures of people dying unnoticed, body after body piling up. I had no idea what it would mean for the relatively fit and almost young like us, but I was honest with the team that the safest thing would be to run and stay inside until it was all over. No one wanted that.

My fear was if I caught it, it might not go so well for me – two bouts of cancer behind me and a bad case of pneumonia six months before whilst on exercise gave me worry. I talked to my wife Lucy about it.

'If I get it and I have to go in...'

'Do we have to talk about this?'

'Yes. There are people dying alone.'

'Lovely!'

'I won't be alone. I'll conjure you. I'll imagine you into being there. If you know this, then it will help.'

'I don't want to talk about this.'

'It'll help me. If you know this.'

'Go to sleep.'

As it was of course, it didn't kill the likes of me. Not in any great numbers. It took our grandparents, and those who had rushed back to help and work in hospitals. It would strike without logic in a young man here, a mother there: but mostly it just made us all sick: wheezy and tired.

But I worried about Eric dying alone.

I lent in.

We sent two Opera North violinists to teach him how to Zoom, two dancers to fix his internet connection, whatever the excuse someone else would be dispatched, in the end all the members of the team, to help with one thing or another. Most of them would report back their concern about an internet girlfriend from Thailand or somewhere similar. When he called with a problem with his smoke alarm, I knew it was time to confront the situation.

I had expected to get through my theatre career without having to bring up the delicate subject of whether an eighty-three-year-old was being taken for a fool by the promise of a young exotic girlfriend. I didn't have a handbook for such discussions, so I buggered on through.

'Have you ever met her?'

'No.'

'Do you give her money?'

'Sometimes.'

'A lot?'

'I don't have a lot.'

'Eric mate, I don't think you should go on with it.'

'Why?' He was upset now.

'I... I... I don't think she's real.'

'Does it matter? She makes me happy.'

It didn't matter a bit, I decided. I fixed his smoke alarm and left. We never spoke about it again. But he would ring me. Nearly every other day for most of the year. Normally before 8am as I drove along the motorway on the way to work and he would chunter on about his days in the RAF or his recent work with the cancer charity. He'd often talk to my young boy Davidbaby in the back of the car, tell tall tales of the picnic we would all have with him when this whole thing was over.

We couldn't find him for a few days into 2021 and then he called one Saturday afternoon.

'I'm in the hospice, Al.'

'Oh Eric.'

'End of life care now.'

'They looking after you pal?'

'Oh yes, lovely nurses.'

'You need anything?'

'Wispa Bites, if you've the time.'

'I've the time Eric.'

'Send the girls. You're busy. Send the girls.'

He'd be dead in a week and I was caught surprised by how upset it made me. Eric had been likeable, which had helped, but he had also been an eye opener for me on the state of the world. That a man like Eric, served in the forces, done well in his life, could find himself alone and disconnected in the way he was upset me. Over the year we would grow good, if not expert, at finding, packing and delivering tonnes of food. I haven't met the majority of the people we deliver to, I don't know their issues beyond the need for food, never mind do anything about them. We are the people with the finger in the dam hoping, hope against all experience and evidence, that someone upstream is doing something to make the situation better in the long run.

But with Eric, and a handful of others, we found the time to care deeply about the details: the internet connection and what it meant to him, the brand of denture fixing, Wispa Bites. He was our friend. A friend made entirely because we promised to do something we didn't understand. Someone that we would never have had any impact on, no matter how many plays we put on at the club. But thanks to Covid he had become our friend. And then one dreary day in January he was dead.

A CHIP ON MY SHOULDER AS
BIG AS A PIANO

During the Covid crisis I was asked to do a lot of speeches at conferences and to groups. No matter what the group, the question was always the same, why are you doing this? And I answer more or less with the section you can find in the Chapter entitled What We Believe.

But that's why Slung Low do what we do. A group of artists determinedly working on a mission, set by values and responding creatively to the world as it happens around them.

But that's not why I do this. I do this for revenge, provoked by the hot sting of embarrassment decades old. I do this because of the chip on my shoulder. I've never met anyone who drives change who doesn't have a chip, and this is mine:

I was born in West Berlin. My father was in the Royal Air Force. Signals. I grew up on a military base called RAF Gatow. Which is basically a walled village – complete with its own shop, its own churches, schools the whole kit and caboodle. All behind the Iron Curtain and surrounded by a large military fence. West Berlin – a part of an older culture war.

In RAF Gatow, it was the case that children who wanted to learn to play the piano could have the loan of one of the instruments held in a central store on the base. I figure this was a practical issue of having all those families moving around the world each lugging a piano after them. Easier to do it this way. In any case, this was a service that was offered – some compensation to living with a Soviet Tank Division within walking distance I would think.

So, my mother goes to the piano office and asks, 'Can I have a piano for my son please?' and she gets the answer – 'Well no, they are for the children of officers.'

The RAF – like the Army and the Navy – are split into ranks. Obviously – it's the armed forces. There are officers who command people to do things. And then there are non-officers who actually do things. My father was a non-officer. He was a Corporal. We've all seen films, we know what corporal means.

And the pianos were for the sons and daughters of officers.

My mother says to the piano man, 'Okay they are normally for officer families sure, but we could make an exception, he's a precocious kid, he's really into the piano, there are spare pianos on base. Please.'

The piano office guy looks at my mother and he says, 'Look, there's no point getting your son's hopes up. Don't be giving him ideas above his station. It's not like he will be able to make a living out of it.'

We talk often about how the foodbank was actually a piece of storytelling – the story was that no one in Holbeck and Beeston would go hungry during the Covid crisis and the easiest way to tell the story was to make it real. Ward-wide storytelling.

Stories matter. They remind us of why we do things. And they help you keep angry for decades when the anger is what helps you keep going.

There are children in Holbeck without crayons. Living in a city with an opera company. An opera company paid for with money from all of us. Until everyone has crayons no one gets opera. That's what I believe. Pianos for everyone, or no one.

And the people of Holbeck deserve the best possible cultural life. And it's our job at Slung Low to do what we can to make that true.

HIGH QUALITY CCTV:
PETE'S CONCLUSION

So, there's some stuff that surprised me about The Holbeck. I expected the toilets to be a 1980's nightmare and they are. The carpet was exactly what you'd imagine in the concert room of the oldest working men's club in Britain. But the quality of the fire alarm was a surprise. It's a brilliant thing – ringing you on your mobile to let you know the place is ablaze. Which is reassuring in a way.

Because it had been run by volunteers for so long, and supported by various little grants and opportunities but never with actual long term investment or regular income, there are little pockets of the gleaming alongside areas not touched for decades, because they are no one's personal priority. So we have an amazing professional kitchen at the club – the result of a grant from the local councillor – complete with soup urns and catering size bain-maries – and the men's urinals smell like a dolphin has died in the pipes no matter what you pour down them to try and fix it. The internet is surprisingly good and WIFI is routed throughout the building, because someone's son-in-law works for an internet company. But the speaker system for bingo announcements would give that one from *M*A*S*H* a run for its money.

And the CCTV is unbelievably good, better coverage than a London underground station and in glorious HD.

Which is why if you were here now looking at the screen behind the bar, you'd be able to see a very highly defined picture of Pete coming to the door one day after deliveries and talking to one of the team. And then another picture of one of us explaining to Pete he was to go round the side of the building to the snooker room door where we load food parcels in and out.

And another picture of Pete pretending to exit through the door but doubling back once the coast was clear and into the office.

And finally, a picture of Pete leaving the building with the foodbank cash box from the office clutched to his chest.

I had to admire the fact that, having stashed the cash box in his bag, he then went round to the snooker room door and took his food parcel. Calm under pressure. An admirable virtue.

Because it was the food bank cash box we use for solving all the problems that come our way that a loaf of white sliced won't solve but £20 might, it was not only full of cash but also handwritten receipts for tasks – '£20 electricity for family with two babies', '£20 for pampers for Mama J's new baby' and so on. We found ourselves in the embarrassing situation of not even knowing how much we had had stolen.

It was somewhere near the £400 mark – certainly enough to pay off the armed drug dealers and plenty more for recreational crack.

It was foolish laziness. I had been caught up in the pace and hurry of the deliveries. It had been my decision to take the cash box out of the safe – too busy racing from problem to solution to be opening the club's old secret agent safe eight times a day with its 'turn the dial clockwise three times, anticlockwise four times'. It had also been hubris after long months of achievement and positivity. Who would rob a food bank? Who would dare come into the oldest working men's club in Britain, now a foodbank, and rob us?

Well, Pete would.

The impact was large. Not the money – that was replaced by our endlessly supportive Twitter followers in moments – but the impact it had on our sense of selves and those we were helping. Even I am not so arrogant to think we were more powerful than crack, but this incident confirmed it starkly and left exposed the limitations of what we could do for the most desperate of our community.

I couldn't blame Pete. He had multiple needs, nearly all of which were beyond our capabilities – many of which were beyond the capabilities of those services we could refer him to.

We didn't see him again for two months. I assumed he'd killed himself with a windfall of crack. But then one wintry February morning there he was.

'Can I get some help with my electricity Alan, it's freezing.' The police had finally been called and apparently gone in with guns and he had got his flat back.

We talked about how, since we'd last talked, the foodbank had been robbed. 'Disgusting Alan, scumbags! It'll be that Darren.'

And how I really wanted to talk to who had done it. 'Take Darren round the back and give them a hiding Alan!'

And how this old pub had state-of-the-art CCTV and every step from the door to the office was covered. 'I am cold and hungry Alan, can I get some help?'

And of course he could, because in what world were we willing to live in where he couldn't.

And so, Sally sat with him on the phone to the people who try to help with electricity and then to the LWSS and Matt fetched him a sleeping bag out of the club bedroom and Ruth Middleton packed up his food in bags for him to carry back to his recently liberated flat.

As he was leaving, he turned back to me and, with the Princess Di expression that is so common in this group of broken men, asked, 'Can you spare me a couple of quid so I can get a little bit.'

I gave him the money I had in my pocket.

I went back to the board of addresses for delivery and sent the next wave of drivers out into the city. Some days there are no good decisions, and you do the least worse one and hope you forget by bedtime.

SIDE BEFORE SELF EVERY TIME

'Good morning, Alan.'

I look up at the greeting and see before me the entirely unexpected sight of a woman in her fifties wearing a full Leeds United Football kit, including socks. Pulled up.

This is Liz. Liz joined us as a driver at first half-way through the year. A brilliant lighting designer, she'd heard about us from friends in the arts and Leeds United Twitter. She was the biggest Leeds United fan, passionate about the club and proud as it increasingly took its social responsibility more seriously than it had under previous leadership.

But we've many fans of the club who volunteer and none of them have ever come to help in a full strip. I wondered what was going on.

People volunteer for all sorts of reasons. Some because it helps them feel less guilty about how fortunate they are. Some because it's a good excuse to get out of the house. Some because their personal morality demands that they do, or their faith provokes them. And some come because it's a place they can belong.

As the year 2020 went on, we were finding more and more of our volunteers were coming because it was giving them a grounding they weren't getting anywhere else. And whilst we understood our responsibilities entirely around the volunteers, one of which was to provide this sense of grounding and routine and connection in lockdowns that had none of that, we were also aware of the dangers of volunteers staying too long.

There's a pattern. People arrive and they are a little bit nervous. They're out the house for the first time in ages, they don't know what to expect. So, we quickly orientate them – explain what we do, how they fit into the system, what to expect. And that trepidation turns into some excitement, a galvanising purpose as they set out to be useful.

Then they grow comfortable, enjoy themselves, start to find it easier, and that confidence allows them to guide others, show the newbies the ropes.

And that wears off and they start to make their efficiencies – little adjustments to their personal systems to make the job a little easier, or a little quicker.

Then the satisfaction starts to wane just a little. Maybe you deliver to the same family a few weeks on the trot and you start to ask the question, is this going to go on forever? The excitement of helping has now subsided and you are left with that nub of usefulness to keep you motivated.

So, you start to question the system, imagine large potential efficiencies in the whole. It's completely natural, but what you can't know from your position in the machine is that some things are necessary to keep the whole thing going. For every four deliveries The Real Junk Food Project brings, one will be food, for a host of reasons, that will be incredibly hard for us to distribute. It might be wholesale soft fruit, out of date bread or something else that is hard to shift, time consuming to sort. Why are we doing this, you'll hear the volunteers say, as they pick through the first of forty large crates of blueberries. And it's hard to understand that this is the cost of the other three deliveries, that being a reliable positive enthusiastic recipient of whatever Adam Smith and TRJFP has is our USP in a world of increasingly picky charities and organisations. It makes up for our lack of cash.

And so, their system manager tendencies thwarted, they start to examine the mission. They return back with reports of people still being in bed, nice cars in drives, piles of cereal boxes in the kitchen and so on. The mood starts to sour.

Time and time again we saw it with people. It's a natural response to both the challenges of lockdowns stretching away in front of you and being one of the fingers in the dam – you start to wonder how bad would it be if you took finger out? I mean is the dam even doing anything?

We learnt, after the first few months, that we needed to put in breaks, or reorganise volunteers as they started to reach the end of their natural enthusiasm. Bringing them inside to pack for a few days, mixing up food deliveries with some arts project or just telling them to have a couple of weeks off would all make a big difference in keeping the pool of volunteers present, happy and content.

And some needed more from us than we were initially prepared to give. For some, our little gang at the club became more important than we were ready for.

And that presented itself in all sorts of ways; volunteers turning up early, staying late; finding ways to get into the bits of the organisation that had nothing to do with foodbanks or delivery. We came to understand that our responsibility to the volunteers was not that dissimilar to those we had to our referrals. We knew the logistical effort needed to manage and care for those volunteers, but the emotional effort became clear as the year went on. These were our people, they were going through a lot – unemployment, isolation – and it was our job to care for them too.

In time we arranged for lunch to be catered by our brilliant friends at Manjit's Kitchen so people could sit and eat together after deliveries, which was a really useful release for many of them, and a programme of training and sessions with an occupational therapist to help people through the challenges of lockdowns.

When Liz read an article I wrote, suggesting that until all children had access to crayons no one should have access to ballet (a predictably bullish answer to the inequalities of arts funding) she came in the next day with one hundred packs of crayons to add to the food parcels. This was Liz.

She had started delivering as a driver, but she was not well and after a few months she could no longer carry the crates of food to the car. She was angry at her weakness, although we all reassured her that there were other ways to contribute: it's a team sport, this foodbank game. She packed bags for a few weeks until she grew frustrated and then one day she appeared in the club in a full Leeds United strip, including socks.

I wondered what was going on.

FOOTBALL FANS AND TOYS
FOR CHRISTMAS

Ewan Metcalfe runs Forging Futures, a programme of training for kids who have fallen out of education or training. It partners with the big property developer CEG, who are building the big new office block on the wasteland between Holbeck and the city centre. Ewan puts the trainees through a series of courses and training and then leverages his connections to secure them a working placement on a building site. Ewan feels like part of this new Leeds energy that seems to have filled the city in the last decade. Tough, caring, unpretentious but with ambition to both enjoy his life and have a positive impact on others. He is part wide boy northern Danny Dyer, part robust socially engaged entrepreneur of a northern powerhouse not of the Government's making. Which is why we're so happy to host the lessons Forging Futures run down in Holbeck – it feels like a good fit. We understand Ewan, we understand the pupils he brings in and mostly they understand us. And learning how to fix your CV or basic maths, or health and safety is a little easier a task if you're doing it sat in a closed pub, a more relaxed environment.

Amongst his other ventures he was part of a Leeds Union football supporters podcast called Roaring Peacocks. He and his European-based partner-in-crime Adonis approached us with an idea. A toy drive. A fundraising effort to raise money from football fans to provide toys to those that might not be receiving many this year.

It was the focus we needed in the run up to Christmas, and a new mission to engage those who had grown a little weary of the relentless food parcel deliveries into the winter.

Their initial target was quickly met and they raised it a number of times until they had enough for 300 new toys.

Now we had to work out how to identify the children. We told the drivers they could nominate any family they were delivering to, but the reality was that it's hard to make a decision like that based on a few seconds on the doorstep. We were going to need experts.

Mercifully we could always rely on the brilliant Kidz Klub and Ingram Road Primary. They created lists of names, ages and addresses. 300 kids who were unlikely to be having a very bountiful Christmas.

Now we knew how many toys we needed and for what age group. There began a pained cultural conversation about whether the toys would be gendered. Pragmatism won out – 'we'll try to dismantle the patriarchy another day, let's just get the kids toys that they might actually want' – and Lucy was dispatched in the company van to buy the right amount of boy and girl toys in the various age groups.

Then they were all wrapped, boxed up into households and ready to be delivered in the two-week run up to Christmas. Leeds United fans came from all over the city to deliver the toys.

'You need sweets at Christmas,' Liz had announced as we were finishing the wrapping and the next day she had arrived with 300 plastic bags full of sweets to go out with the toys. And the next week there she stood in a full Leeds United strip, complete with socks. Pulled up.

'I'm going to be in charge of the toy room, handing them out. It's too much for you to do on your own.'

It wasn't. The plan was working fine. Ruth M had taken over organising the food delivery drivers – now up to 300+ parcels a week – and I directed the Roaring Peacocks and their toy deliveries. But I also knew that Liz was determined to do this.

She no longer had the strength to take food parcels or toys out on deliveries and the sweets had been a generous, kind and forceful declaration of her continued usefulness.

'Of course Liz, let me take you through what needs to happen.'

With the strip on and holding some wrapped toys we took some photos for social media and she spent the days that week assigning toys to drivers as they came from being given their addresses.

At the end of the week, we closed the food bank for Christmas and began preparations for our Christmas show. I wouldn't see Liz again.

She was very ill and she would die in the Christmas holidays.

Those last few days, doling out toys dressed in her team's colours were important to her, I think. She wanted this. And we were able to provide it.

She was the clearest example of something that we knew to be true of so many of the brilliant, heroic, kind and useful people who volunteered with us. The engine of the whole system. We needed them. But they needed us nearly as much.

HOW DID OUR NAME GET IN THEIR MOUTH?

There was a two-month period in the middle of it all when we were the darlings of the arts sector. The great and the good would go on Radio 4 and talk about what an amazing job Slung Low in *checks notes* Holbeck, Leeds was doing.

I was driving in one morning listening to the radio and heard the big commercial producer Sonia Friedman was talking about how fab we were.

In all these speeches the next sentence was always to demand the government give money, more money, to the arts sector to help them through. I wondered how much of that money we at *checks notes* Slung Low would get. I wondered how much of it would make its way to the freelance artists and workers who were the below the waterline iceberg of the whole sector.

It would turn out in time that we would do all right. Those freelancers less so.

But nonetheless for about two months we, along with the theatre in Pitlochry and the Battersea Arts Centre and a handful of others, were the darlings of the news stories. It's happened to us before. It never lasts long, it's not to be taken seriously.

'Do any of you lot know Sonia Friedman?' I asked one day in the office.

'Who?' says a Ruth.

'Well, that answers that.'

'Why?' asks Joanna.

'She's mentioned us a few times on the radio and stuff, I don't know her.'

'Is it a problem?'

'No. We're getting used for political cover so they don't have to talk about the arts organisations who had done bugger all, but I don't think it makes any difference. I just want to know how our name ended up in her mouth.'

One of the results of this was a hundred invitations to speak. People wanted to know about what we were doing, why and what difference it might make to the future. I did at least four speeches or Q & As a week for half a year.

The upside to these moments of surge is that you get to talk about your values, about why you're doing something and the impact you hope it might have. And you charge people. We made thousands in speech fees and every penny bought some beans that we could send out the next day. And the more I spoke, the more donations we got online as the story spread.

The downside is you keep telling your story and you see the world not changing and it has a strange demoralising effect. Day in, day out, you hope something in a speech changes something in the world. And of course it doesn't, and again the next day and the next day. And it grinds you down.

Peculiarly there are many that respond to your story as if it is a personal attack. Like our story is that everyone should be doing what we're doing. It doesn't matter if you say that isn't the case, there is always someone on the call who, through guilt or just playing devil's advocate or because they really believe it, will push back or diminish your efforts and knock away at your resolve. Every single time.

I don't know whether this is a feature of the arts sector or not, but it was telling that the response was always warmer, more welcoming in other fields: telling the story to accountants, or business managers, or soldiers was a substantially nicer experience.

Towards the end of the year, early December, I was doing a speech for some northern arts leaders and the first question was, 'why are you bothering with all this?'

I was tired. I had watched *Scrooged* the night before. And I didn't like the tone of this man, so I answered, 'I'm trying to save my soul, what are you doing?'

It was meant to be a joke. It didn't land as a joke. The call quickly moved on and the mercy of Zoom means I have no idea how this dude responded to my condemnation of his soul, but it checked me.

I couldn't go on like this. All of us working flat out on the foodbank two thirds of the day, dealing with chaotic food supply and then trying to run a theatre company in the remaining time. And trying to fit in Ghost of Christmas future Zoom speeches on a daily basis. Something was going to snap.

In the new year we would need a new plan.

We'd remain committed to being a non-means tested self-referral food bank. Anyone who wanted food could have it. But we'd need to organise ourselves more to focus our energy and the volunteers' energy. And we'd need a food supply more consistent than the many strands we currently had which required daily herding.

Mercifully the Council had proposed increasing the funding. Previously it had been £5k every three months, and that had grown to £8k every three months. Now they were proposing £41k for six months. Until June 2021 is what they wanted. It wouldn't cover the actual costs of the operation, but it would get a lot closer than previously.

It was decided. In the new year we would move operations to one day a week. It would galvanise our volunteers and reduce burn out. It would free up three days a week of the Slung Low team to do our actual jobs. But we'd need to start buying in wholesale food to supplement our pals at The Real Junk Food

Project and other free supplies. And that would cost us more. But it would help us keep going in the long run.

300 deliveries in a single day. It was possible but it would be hard graft. This was our fifth system of the crisis. We had confidence we could make it work. A new plan for the new year.

And something had to change. We were too knackered to go on as we were. I was too tightly strung – I couldn't go around the place threatening people's souls. It was time for this new plan. And to re-find my sense of humour. Or at least a sense of hope.

WHY DOES A THEATRE COMPANY RUN A FOODBANK?

We've already talked about how we spend public money on the arts in this country and that means every part of it should get to experience some of that culture. That's why we are in Holbeck and that's why we are Pay What You Decide.

And this is a moral imperative.

And let's imagine we are putting on a great cabaret in the car park. Fantastic acts, a band, dinner in the middle. And it's Pay What You Decide, so financial standing is no obstacle to attending.

And in one, or many, but let us imagine in one of the 200 houses and flats in line of sight and hearing of the club there is a woman. Let us imagine her as a zero-hour contract cleaner with two kids, on her own in a small house. Doing her best. And she doesn't know where she's going to get the kids' breakfast from tomorrow. And imagine the panic that causes in her chest. That rising panic dominating her mind, limiting her choices. Frantically thinking what she can do. Who can she call? Where can she go?

And then she hears a noise – it's a band starting up. The show is going to start.

There's no godly way she can possibly come to that show. That show becomes an act of aggression. A taunting, noisy disturbance.

What started off as a moral imperative becomes an act of cultural aggression, an insensitivity that flows from the most cardinal of sins for professional artists – a lack of imagination.

We know that people are in this situation. We know that some of those people live in our community. And to do nothing about it because 'it's not our fault' is the sort of excuse that people have always used to let themselves off the hook for not doing the difficult thing. It isn't our fault. But it is our responsibility. It isn't only our responsibility, nor our only responsibility. But it is *our* responsibility.

How was I going to put a big old, joyful show on in the middle of a pandemic whilst people went hungry as they stared at the stage from their homes? Who would that make us?

And that's the answer I gave them every time they asked. It was the only way that we could put our shows on in clear conscience. The foodbank was the only way we could possibly justify the theatre.

YOU CAN BET

The National Student Drama Festival is little known outside of the arts sector, but has supported the early development of Stephen Fry, Meera Syal, Simon Russell Beale, Rik Mayall, Pete Postlethwaite, Wole Soyinka and a whole galaxy of stars. And us.

When we were kids our minds were blown by the talent of other students at different universities who gathered at the NSDF. We were the only theatre freaks in our university and it was so galvanising to discover that there were people like us all over the country. NSDF allowed all of us to gather for one week a year to share our shows.

We'd stayed involved over the twenty years since we were there as kids and supported the festival, now run by our long-standing collaborator and dear friend, the playwright James Phillips, with prize money and what resources we could spare.

And then a few weeks just before NSDF20 the nation locked down. James decided he was taking it online and we offered our support.

He wondered whether we could contribute something to the social aspect that was usually such an important part of the festival; something fun and frivolous.

At the same time, we were hearing from the Sunday drinking club members about how they were missing their bingo and general natter. As a group they weren't much for the digital interaction, which was all the rage in lockdown one. However, they were prolific users of Facebook.

We started to imagine a live, interactive gameshow on Facebook. Matt set about finding the streaming equipment we'd need. It was a one-off so hard to justify spending too much money on it but at the same time we had a reputation to protect: we'd won a Royal Television Society Yorkshire award for *Flood* so we couldn't just bung some mobile phone footage up online.

In the end, Matt would create a three camera, radio microphoned set-up, which made everything look like shiny floor television from the early 80s. And that was perfect for what we were planning.

In the 90s there was a particularly entertaining Saturday night TV show called *You Bet!* It was hosted by Matthew Kelly, the nicest man in professional showbusiness. Contestants would declare unlikely skills – correctly guess the sex of 100 goldfish in two minutes, move a tea set by radio-controlled model helicopter and so on. The live audience would guess whether the guest could achieve it or not. Then they would try to do it.

We would recreate this gameshow on Facebook. Those watching at home (members of the oldest working men's club in Britain and drama students together) would ring in to a special number and guess whether the challenges could be achieved.

And then I would try and do the challenges in the studio. Simple!

The only other people who could come into the theatre with lockdown regulations were my wife Lucy and our five-year-old son Davidbaby: they'd have to do the other parts of the challenges that needed a second person.

And so, we set about pulling together the show. The first challenge was shooting a plastic tomato off the head of Matt with a NERF gun whilst blindfolded. The second was throwing Davidbaby (in full safety gear) over an ironing board on to a beanbag crash mat. The third was a contestant from home identifying the make and model of cars just by the sound of their door slamming.

With days to go, we realised that we'd never get permission to use the title *You Bet!* And Facebook was notoriously unrelaxed about these things, so we changed the title to *You Can Bet*.

It was a one-off to help our pal James and as ropey as it was starting to feel, it would surely do.

In the end it would more than do. It proved to be wildly popular, creating the sort of local community, niche sector connection activity that a thousand Zoom pub quizzes were achieving all over the country. Members sat at home on Facebook heckling in the comment box along with actors in LA and drama students all over the country.

Matthew Kelly kindly filmed a to-camera piece, fake-furious at how we'd ripped off his format which added an air of showbiz. The theme tune was Jamie Fletcher's 'Club at the Edge of Town' which had proved so popular when her band had played it at the opening cabaret over a year before; that added a sense of polish.

It would come back every fortnight during the first lockdown and feature more and more of Davidbaby as Stunt Supervisor David Anthony Bevan Lane, with challenges as daft as cutting logs with a chainsaw blindfolded, and wearing a zorb whilst a golfer tried to hit me with a golf ball from 50m away.

When the first lockdown started to lift, a drive-in version was simultaneously streamed online, much to the delight of the audience in their cars who spent the show beeping their horns endlessly.

And our first big show back live was a version of *You Can Bet* in the car park on a lorry stage complete with fireworks and live band.

This silly gameshow, with its starring role for a five-year-old boy in a high visibility vest, proved the spine for our year. As the foodbank ramped up and took on ever increasing output this was our way of reminding ourselves (and others) that we were a theatre company. If our funders didn't need reminding, sometimes we did.

We knew the year needed to end, not only with a bang, but also coherently. We had managed to constantly evolve and react as 2020 had battered our community (and us). At every point we had delivered the practical support everyone needed but also the creative support.

LS11 Art Gallery had reminded everyone that they weren't just scared, they could be other things too.

Shows for families and the school in the middle of the year had reminded everyone of the robustness the arts can bring, and the need for young people to be told stories that weren't full of despair.

The foodbank would shut for Christmas week. We had to mark the change and remind people of what we were about, of what we had done together these last nine months.

You Can Bet It's Christmas was the answer. Written by the brilliant Lisa Holdsworth, a very non-festive host Alan began the gameshow as usual but was almost immediately interrupted by a couple, Yusef and Mariam, who were expecting their baby any moment now and had nowhere to stay. After they were offered the flat above the club, the gameshow continued but keeps getting interrupted by elements of the nativity; the Shepherd family who have bought some basics for Yusef and Mariam; midwives arriving angelically; and finally, three wise Yorkshire women stopping in on their way to the bingo. The Scrooge-like host tries to keep the show on the road.

In the final moments the wise women conjured up the mottos of our year in neon signs on the side of the building.

No one knew we had got this done, so it was surprise to all the volunteers and foodbank recipients in the live audience and online when three big bright red signs lit up the side of the building:

Be kind. Be useful. We go again tomorrow, pals.

The three phrases that had got us through the year, that had become such an important, rallying call as our friends and supporters had sought to keep us going, especially through the tough and demanding November and December months.

All three to see there on the side of the building. Bright like a guiding star. This was what we had been doing all year long. Storytelling best we can.

The show was a hit. People left weeping with festive spirit ready for their Christmas break.

We waved goodbye to people live and online as we stripped away the stage and lighting.

Darren arrived just as we were nearing the last job.

'Can I get a food parcel Al?'

'We shut three days ago Darren, we did talk about this.'

'Please.'

There's no food left in the club. The place is empty for Christmas. I look at him standing there with his friend and go to the office. I return with a handful of cash.

'Here you go Darren, shops will still be open tomorrow. Get yourself some Christmas.' I hand them forty quid each. Small price to pay to enjoy my Christmas day without guilt.

Word will spread quickly and soon his mates will be down looking for the idiot handing out forty quid, but we'll all be gone in two hours.

Be useful, be kind. But for once after nine months' hard graft we wouldn't go again tomorrow.

There was one last job of the year before a week's break. The neon sign had to come down. If we left the neon up unattended it'd get smashed with a thrown stone within days.

I DON'T WANT A LOT FOR CHRISTMAS

There are a few perks to being a governor and definitely the thing I was looking forward to most was visiting on Christmas Lunch Day. Towards the end of term, the school canteen plans a Christmas lunch and guests come in to eat with the kids.

Because of Covid they were all in their classrooms but that did not dint my excitement.

We immediately started a 'Mariah Carey' competition with renditions of 'All I Want for Christmas' and moved on to cracker jokes. I haven't laughed that much in a long time as the kids shared theirs and rolled their eyes at the terrible jokes I'd brought along.

Then it was time for lunch. Everyone who got Free School Meals or who opted into the school meal system got a tray of turkey, trimmings and vegetables. But there was still plenty of kids who brought their own packed lunch in: for cultural reasons perhaps, or for dietary ones, or simply because they liked cheese sandwiches made by their parents. There are other reasons too.

The girl in front of me had a packed lunch box, a soft shell one like my son has, which I noticed she quietly slid onto the desk before placing her jumper over it.

I was getting on with my veggie sausages and stuffing balls, both of which could magnificently be used as buck shot if you were looking to hunt turkeys – like your nanna used to make – when the girl, we'll call her Sophie because that's not her name, when Sophie quietly unzipped the lunch box then put her hand back on her lap. A few second later Sophie put her hand inside the lunch box and just left it there. What was she doing?

Then, after a few moments pause, the hand shot up to her mouth and back into the lunch box.

I kept chewing my never-ending stuffing balls, and sat quietly watching Sophie, trying to work out what she was doing.

On one of the little dashes her hand made to her mouth, she knocked open her lunch box so I saw for a second what was in it. It was half a Styrofoam tray with a handful of French fries and a half-eaten piece of fried chicken.

She was eating like this, her little dormouse action, because she didn't want people to see what she had for lunch. A few more hand grabs and the lunch box was away, 'yes miss, finished miss' and she was back smiling and laughing with her friends, 'I don't want a lot for Christmasssssssss.'

We talked a lot about how what we were doing during Covid, and particularly the non-means tested foodbank, was a finger in the dam. And our hope was that there were some smart people further upstream doing something really clever and original, that meant we could at some point take our finger out of the hole.

I didn't until that moment really understand how much water was coming downstream. We had, within the small community of Holbeck at least, made it known that whoever needed healthy, fresh, free food could have it. We had done this in many languages, through every partner conceivable: we had demonstrated the strength of our conviction and promise by doing it even for those to who mocked the simplicity of our offer. We had done this for months, every single day, for thousands of deliveries to hundreds of homes. To whoever asked.

And I had nurtured in my heart the vain thought that all this would mean that, within the two thousand or so households of Holbeck, no child would go hungry. That no child would have to eat the leftover cold chips and gnawed chicken of yesterday. It isn't much that vanity, but it was enough to keep me going through the many months of deliveries and finding food and money. That little boast, always made internally, never out loud. But still.

And it wasn't true.

It was false because, as Adam Smith said, food poverty, poverty generally, is a political problem. And we only had practical, logistical tools at our disposal to deal with this political problem. And, like putting in a nail with a saw, it won't solve the problem.

We could do our bit. But we would always be a finger in the dam. The systemic failings that led to a handful of cold French fries for a young girl's lunch were beyond the reach of a foodbank, however well run, however ambitious, however much we told our story and strove to achieve.

One of the biggest contributors to food poverty in Holbeck is the hostile environment. Which of course isn't an accidental outcome of a deregulated jobs market, like zero-hour contracts in a global pandemic; or delays in administrative processing of benefits, like the introduction of universal benefit system. All of which are destructive and appalling but at least have the scant excuse of being outcomes of a system designed to achieve something else.

No, the hostile environment is an active policy to make some people's lives unpleasant. To rob them of the time, space, and resources needed to be comfortable. It's a policy designed to make you panic and to harry you along your life with just enough tension for the environment to feel, well, hostile. It's a policy designed to ensure your kids eat a handful of cold French fries for lunch.

And it was only vanity in my heart that made me think, if only for a few months, only within a small neighbourhood, that maximum effort and total commitment could overcome that cruelty.

That lunchtime visit was one of the most joyous things I did during the whole Covid crisis. Thirty kids from a whole variety of different backgrounds joined as one in their joyful glee at renditions of Mariah Carey's Christmas hit. And contained within that precious hour the saddest realisation about the limit of what we could do. And the cruelty we visit on those who deserve it the least.

It hardened my heart that moment. Not against the brilliant children of Holbeck. Nor those who were new arrivals to Britain, seeking a better life in the back-to-back red brick terraced housing of South Leeds. No, it hardened my heart to those who had done this, consciously and unconsciously in their appealing to the worst of us with these policies. They had done this and they had done it on purpose.

WHAT'S THE HARDEST THING
ABOUT IT ALL?

One day Matt, one of the contemporary Friar Tucks from before, comes round with the head of his church handing out chocolates to the neighbourhood. It's the new year, so we've moved to one day a week. A weak January sun is setting, so we've finished the 300 deliveries that we now do in a frantic four-hour dash with three dozen volunteers. I'm tired, Davidbaby is running around somewhere, adding stress and joy in equal measure, and most frustratingly we are entering our fourth attempt in two weeks to get regular referral Darren sorted with his benefits.

Darren is a lost soul, profound mental health issues: his phone doesn't work, his flat burnt down, he's in and out of hospital and at least once every ten days he turns up at the club telling me can't cope any more with the challenges he's facing and he's going to top himself. He's been referred to every single adult, mental and social health number we could find and none of them make a blind bit of difference.

Faced with this seemingly impossible situation repeating on us over and over, I become determinedly practical.

Let us focus on getting this man his benefits, get information flowing through to him, fix his phone, then we'll worry about the bigger problems. Which means over the last two weeks various members of the team, first Sally, then Kara, our dramaturg from the University of Leeds, throw themselves on the challenge with the instruction to ring the benefits people and be as middle-class as they can.

The benefits system is confusing even for a university academic with a doctorate – every conversation starts from the assumption that Darren is lying, it makes no assumption of good faith, and it is cruel in its deafness to his demonstrable pain and torment. And more importantly we don't seem to be able to make a blind bit of difference. I've popped the Hulk suit back on, hoping to smash the mess into a different configuration and send a series of emails designed to shock the system into action.

At the same time, I'm aware that Darren can't even be trusted to take £20 to the shop to buy himself the electricity that he will stand weeping outside my office telling me he needs. The man's mind is fractured, it's hard to pull out the coherent information, let alone get the same story two tellings in a row. Is this the hill I'm willing to die on? What I've learnt about the benefits system over the last year is not much, is this really the moment to go all in on trying to shake the system loose?

But I know this to be true:

Darren is due £600 a month. Not having that money is making him suicidal. And no amount of playing the game, helping him through the system, well-spoken clever people being reasonable is working. So, it's time to get on the front foot, pick up the phone to someone on the benefits line and forcibly explain the impact of both the system and individual's failure to be responsive and rattle a solution out of this knackered system. And I was just getting ready to do exactly that when Matt arrives with his church leader.

They ask if anyone had any pain that needed healing.

'No, you're okay loves, I think everyone is okay today.'

'The builders?' We're using the third lockdown to finally secure wheelchair access to the bar which is why there are four builders outside concreting.

'No, I think they're all very healthy.' I don't know what happens if they try to heal the builders, but I don't have the energy for the fall-out.

We chat about how it's going, the fact that people aren't angry anymore like in the summer, just sad and slow. We've responded by getting creative packs and resources from all our arts buddies – we're getting some lovely feedback about the moments of joy they're bringing.

'Well, it doesn't matter if you don't have any faith, God is very pleased with you. Very pleased with what you are doing.'

I'm not sure what to do with that. What good is his pleasure doing me? Doing Darren? Doing any of them? But these people are my friends, I admire their resolute kindness. I say thank you. And do the shuffling weight thing we do when we're signalling it's time to go. I'm thinking about Darren, about putting the Hulk suit on.

'What is the hardest part of doing this do you think?' The church leader asks almost as an afterthought. In that moment the answer is absolutely clear to me.

When we started out making theatre, the people who had been doing it for a long time told us that we were doing it wrong, that we were naïve to do it the way we were. And we ignored them and after a while everyone agreed that we were doing it right.

When we moved into a venue and we made everything Pay What You Decide and let everyone come and go as they wanted, people who had been running theatres for a long time told us that we were doing it wrong, that we were naïve, that we were putting public money at risk. And we ignored them and after a while everyone agreed that we were doing it right.

When we were making television and we did it our way, the people who been doing it for years told us that we were doing it wrong, that we were naïve, that we were putting public money at risk, that we were dangerous. And we ignored them and then we did it and everyone agreed that we had done it right.

And the same thing when we opened a food bank: that we were doing it wrong, we were naïve, we were putting public money at risk, that we were dangerous, that we would ruin people in the generosity of support. And we ignored them and got on with it. And after a while they gave us a medal for doing it and they put us on their lists of 'good people' and they asked if we could model our activity so others could do what we did.

And the hardest part of doing this is dealing with the fear I have about being wrong with this next challenge. Whatever it is, today it is Darren. And the fear that years of smashing ourselves up against systems designed to keep the status quo in place, years of galvanising the soul to ignore the loud and experienced cries of criticism has actually destroyed my ears. What if I become part of the problem rather than an attempt at a solution?

Certainty has been the best weapon, best advantage for twenty years – the crowbar by which we've made real change in a number of places from an improbably unimpressive starting position. Our certainty has fed thousands of families in moments when they would have otherwise gone hungry. But that certainty will be, I know with other certainty, my undoing eventually.

I draw breath. There's a silence.

I wish them good luck and close the door on the friars. They've salted caramel Lindt chocolate balls to give away to others and I can't use their prayers today. I've a benefits system to wail at.

KEEPING OUR PROMISE

It's Spring 2021. The reopening of the bar is just around the corner. Outdoor theatre shows are already on sale. Foodbank numbers have hit a peak with 400 being delivered every week: we're spending more on food than ever. Talk is beginning with the council about the day when the foodbank has to shut, as it must: what replaces us when we have to go back full-time to something other than tins of baked beans?

The local councillors get in touch to say they've got some of Rishi Sunak's money and if it isn't spent quick it will have to go back. Can we do something on fuel poverty? We set the volunteers to it and distribute over five grand in £20 meter top-ups in just under three weeks. A return to the feeling of Robin Hood vibes we started this whole adventure with.

We've redecorated the bar (same colours as it was just new paint). Ian McMillan's poem beautifully illustrated and hanging on the wall along with images of the different Leeds United supporter groups that used the club as a base and we hope return after lockdown. It looks gleaming. The outside has had a facelift too and now has disabled access for the first time in its long history with a new ramp.

We haven't touched the lounge where bingo is played because we've learnt.

Some of the members come in to have a look at the changes.

'Why haven't you done the lounge?'

'We didn't want to mess with it: I know how particular about it you are.'

'It won't look right now the rest has been done up. It should be painted.'

'Okay.'

'If you organise a date and we'll all come and paint it with you.'

As they are leaving one of them turns back.

'We know that if Slung Low weren't here this place would definitely have closed by now.'

'That's okay, we're just keeping our promise.'

And they're gone. It occurs to me as I get back to work that if they are all coming down, we'll need more paintbrushes.

WE ARE ALL POWERFUL

There's a great and pernicious story told in the last twenty, maybe even forty years, about the nature of power. Or what it is to be powerful.

We are full of stories of Ironman, mega-stars and extraordinary individuals doing extraordinary things in extraordinary moments. We don't tell many stories about groups of people managing to make things together, working together, day in day out to have an impact but we're full of tales of individuals throwing Hail Marys to win the day.

The idea that it is only the individual capable of provoking genuine change in the world, the superhero narrative, is one that keeps most everyone else in a state of not being arsed.

We are all capable of extraordinary power. Each and every ordinary one of us. As a team of ordinaries we are capable of profound impact.

Thirty volunteers deliver 300 boxes of food every week in 2021 from the Slung Low foodbank. We know, we absolutely know, that one of those parcels will reach a house at the end of their capacity. A house that has no food. That feels it has no more options. That is scared of how the children are going to be fed in the morning. And that fear, that rising panic will force out the ability to make good choices, the options will be limited, the fog will come in. And, knowing we have unusually high levels of domestic violence in the ward, maybe that panic becomes a closed fist.

We can be absolutely certain that one of these parcels, maybe more than one but at least for certain one, will arrive at the right moment and that rising panic will dissipate.

That fist can unclench. Those tears do not start. Full bellies go to sleep knowing that in the morning there is breakfast.

A bounce in the step on the way to school. Who knows what happens then?

What moment of learning or realisation happens, because of all that is set in motion by the arrival of a box of food? Or the parent coming home from school drop-off catches a leaflet for an adult education course and thinks, why not? Or anything else that might bring a moment of joy into someone's life.

Maybe all that doesn't happen this week. But next week there's another 300 food boxes and we'll take our chance again with those.

And we know, we don't have to be statisticians to know, that it will happen. The numbers are large enough to ensure that it does.

So those thirty volunteers, all the team at Slung Low, all our partners, and food suppliers, and the gang at Voluntary Action Leeds and the City Council, and all those tens of thousands of donated pounds spent on food, and all that theatre made and funding applied to get that money, and the 150 years of the club being here and every single van of wholesale deliveries emptied box by back-breaking box – all of this – made that moment. That moment of profound change. That moment of panic subsiding and a fist being unclenched and there being just enough room in someone's chest and mind for that glorious moment of realisation, or joy, or learning that might lead anywhere. And isn't that worth it? To be certain that you have given someone a moment's peace, what would you give? What would you do?

Well, for that moment, we'd do all this.

And they have the audacity to think we are not powerful. We are. All of us. Powerful and capable of making real and extraordinary change in the world.

Will the kids sat on their bikes literally in the gutter, watching the opera dress rehearsal in the car park of the club last summer become professional singers? Will one of them? Or will all of them grow up with the great joy of putting on a recording of *Hansel and Gretel* and letting it transport them back to a happy sunny sweaty day when they were young, when they sat in the road and listened transfixed. Will the music of that day bring them comfort as their heart is breaking sometime in the future?

Yes, all of that is capable of being true. Or something so similar to it that it's the same thing.

But we don't get to be there when it happens. That's the rub. That's why you have to carry your certainty with you, why so many in Holbeck ask God to carry theirs for them. Because we won't be there when it happens. When the fist unclenches because of some white bread you unloaded from a van two days before. Or the heart soars in twenty years' time as they listen to an old opera and remember. Or any of the other things that are absolutely a result of the efforts and determination of all those who worked with us through the crisis and did their best. We won't be there. But that doesn't mean they don't happen. It doesn't mean we didn't help them to happen. That we are not powerful, that we are not capable of changing the world one person, one moment at a time.

It's just there'll be no curtain call for all of it, no round of applause. No moment when we look at each other and say, 'we did that' and feel our efforts are worth it. But that doesn't mean we didn't do it. Because we did. And our world changed.

THANKS

At its heart this book is the tale of a large group of people doing difficult things. Where there is achievement, it is theirs, where inadequacies, mine.

Thank you to Paul Hamlyn Foundation and Arts Council England for their money and support. The second making the first even more useful.

Thank you to everyone who supported the foodbank operation: the extraordinary volunteers, magnificent donors, steadfast suppliers and all the staff at Leeds City Council and Voluntary Action Leeds.

Thanks to Tina Leslie at Freedom4Girls, Jeremy Morton at South Leeds Life, Michael Kinsey and John Mallalieu at Leeds United Foundation, Mick Doe at Clipper, the lads at Square Ball, Leeds Bread Cooperative, Mark and Laura Hodgkinson, Martin Dean whilst he was at the council and even more after he left, Ewan Metcalfe with both his Forging Futures and Roaring Peacocks hats on, Adam Smith and all at The Real Junk Food Project, Claire Graham, Rich Hand, Manjit's Kitchen, Cottingley Community Centre, Julie Marshall, Shanaz Gul and all at Hamara, Councillors Gabriel, Scopes and Gohar, Jen Toksvig and everyone else I'll have forgotten.

Sarah Millard and all the staff at Ingram Road Primary School: perfect partners in crime.

Thanks to Amber Maisie-Blomfield, Darren Henley and Tim Etchells for their encouragement and wisdom. Thank you to Kara McKechnie for all the thinking and proofing. Thanks to Abigail Scott Paul and the gang at Leeds 2023 for all their support. Thanks to George Spender and Salamander Street for seeing the potential in the book.

Thanks to James Phillips for his brilliant thoughts on the book and everything else.

To Joanna, Matt and Ruth: it's a team sport or it's nothing. Thank you.

And Lucy. For everything and always.

eCPSIA information can be obtained
at www.ICGtesting.com
Printed in the USA
JSHW042310300422
25465JS00003B/4

9 781914 228414